MEDIEVAL CASTLES
STATELY & HISTORIC HOUSES
OF GREAT BRITAIN & NORTHERN IRELAND

MEDIEVAL CASTLES
STATELY & HISTORIC HOUSES
OF GREAT BRITAIN & NORTHERN IRELAND

FROM ANCIENT TIMES TO THE WARS OF THE ROSES AND 1485

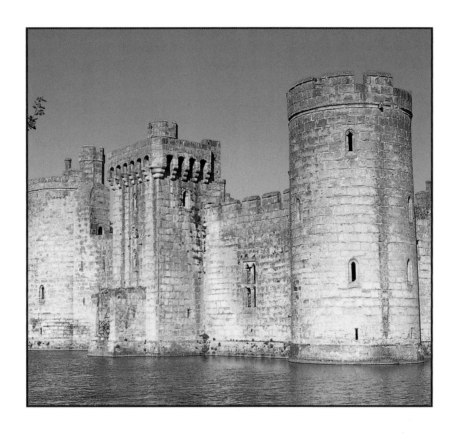

CHARLES PHILLIPS
CONSULTANT: PROFESSOR RICHARD G. WILSON FRHistS

southwater

This edition is published by Southwater an imprint of Anness Publishing Ltd Hermes House
88–89 Blackfriars Road
London SE1 8HA
tel. 020 7401 2077; fax 020 7633 9499

www.southwaterbooks.com;
www.annesspublishing.com

Anness Publishing has a new picture agency outlet for images for publishing, promotions or advertising. Please visit our website www.practicalpictures.com for more information.

UK agent: The Manning Partnership Ltd; tel. 01225 478444; fax 01225 478440; sales@manning-partnership.co.uk

UK distributor: Grantham Book Services Ltd; tel. 01476 541080; fax 01476 541061; orders@gbs.tbs-ltd.co.uk

North American agent/distributor: National Book Network;
tel. 301 459 3366; fax 301 429 5746; www.nbnbooks.com

Australian agent/distributor:
Pan Macmillan Australia; tel. 1300 135 113; fax 1300 135 103; customer.service@macmillan.com.au

New Zealand agent/distributor:
David Bateman Ltd; tel. (09) 415 7664; fax (09) 415 8892

Publisher: Joanna Lorenz
Editor: Joy Wotton
Copy Editor: Alison Bolus
Designer: Nigel Partridge
Illustrators: Anthony Duke, Rob Highton and Vanessa Card
Production Controller: Pirong Wang

ETHICAL TRADING POLICY
At Anness Publishing we believe that business should be conducted in an ethical and ecologically sustainable way, with respect for the environment and a proper regard to the replacement of the natural resources we employ.

As a publisher, we use a lot of wood pulp to make high-quality paper for printing, and that wood commonly comes from spruce trees. We are therefore currently growing more than 750,000 trees in three Scottish forest plantations: Berrymoss (130 hectares/320 acres), West Touxhill (125 hectares/305 acres) and Deveron Forest (75 hectares/185 acres). The forests we manage contain more than 3.5 times the number of trees employed each year in making paper for the books we manufacture.

Because of this ongoing ecological investment programme, you, as our customer, can have the pleasure and reassurance of knowing that a tree is being cultivated on your behalf to naturally replace the materials used to make the book you are holding.

Our forestry programme is run in accordance with the UK Woodland Assurance Scheme (UKWAS) and will be certified by the internationally recognized Forest Stewardship Council (FSC). The FSC is a non-government organization dedicated to promoting responsible management of the world's forests. Certification ensures forests are managed in an environmentally sustainable and socially responsible way. For further information about this scheme, go to www.annesspublishing.com/trees

Previously published as part of a larger volume, *The Complete Illustrated Guide to the Castles, Palaces & Stately Houses of Britain and Ireland*

Page 1: Rochester Castle
Page 2: Conway Castle
Page 3: Bodiam Castle
Page 4 left to right: Edinburgh Castle, Manorbier Castle, Beaumaris Castle
Page 5 left to right: Castle Urquhart, Bodiam Castle, Conway Castle

CONTENTS

INTRODUCTION

In the years after 1066, as the great Norman lords spread out through England and Wales to take control of lands granted them by King William I, they built castles wherever they settled. Castles were immensely effective as instruments of war, for during a siege a small garrison could often hold a great army at bay, yet they were also residences, the proud homes of the new Norman aristocracy. Battlements, gatehouses and turrets became symbols of lordly authority, and men sought to express their wealth and social eminence in stone added fortifications to their country homes. The fortified manor houses they built in the late 14th and the 15th century proclaimed status while combining comfort with security, reaching magnificence with the rise of the Tudor dynasty in 1485.

Left: The original Pembroke Castle was built by Roger, Norman Lord of Dyfed.
William Marshall, Earl of Pembroke, added the cylindrical tower keep (centre) c.1200.

THE AGE OF CHIVALRY

 Castles summon a stirring vision of the past. They have the power to make us dream of mounted knights and their ladies, of jousting in the lists, of fearless swordfighting and the heroic deprivations of siege warfare. When we visit castle sites in England and Wales, we find either evocative ruins or romantic Victorian reconstructions – encouraging us in reveries of the 'age of chivalry'.

No English or Welsh castles survive in their original form from the Middle Ages because they were all either brought to ruin by natural decay, damaged in the fighting of the English Civil War or deliberately slighted (made indefensible) by the victorious Parliamentary army. In Scotland, however, castles survived longer – some played a part in the Jacobite conflicts of the 18th century, when an alliance of highlanders, English rebels and foreign supporters failed in their attempt to restore the House of Stuart to the throne.

One cause of castles' enduring appeal – and the key reason wealthy gentlemen in the 19th and early 20th centuries wanted to rebuild their great country houses with turrets and gatehouses –

Below: The oldest-surviving part of the Tower of London, the White Tower of c.1078, was once painted with whitewash.

is that these fortresses are centuries-old symbols of social status and authority. The castle embodies lordship.

CASTLES AND THE FEUDAL SYSTEM

Castle-building was introduced to England by William the Conqueror and his Norman army in 1066. (A few English castles in Herefordshire and Essex did predate the Conquest, but these were built by Norman friends and associates of Edward the Confessor.) The invaders swept aside the Anglo-Saxon aristocracy, imposing a new Norman ruling class bound to King William I and his descendants by the ties of the feudal system. The castles they built were symbols of feudal authority. They were the fortified homes of knights and great lords, who held them within the feudal system as vassals of the king or as vassals of a superior lord in return for military support and loyal service.

Castles were of course regal as well as lordly residences. Most of the kings of medieval England were great castle-builders, from William I to Edward I and beyond; the most prominent exceptions, Edward II and Richard II, were both victims of the military

Above: Harlech Castle in North Wales, built by Edward I c.1283, has the double defensive walls of the 'concentric castle'.

strength embodied by castles, being slain in castle dungeons. At the Tower of London and Windsor, William I founded great royal strongholds that have endured, with many additions and alterations, to this day as embodiments of royal tradition and pre-eminence.

FROM TIMBER TO STONE

In the early years, most Norman castles were timber and earthwork fortifications. The typical early Norman castle was the 'motte and bailey'. The motte or mound stood within its own defensive barrier, and often supported at its summit a tower containing the lord's living apartments. The bailey was the larger area around the motte, enclosed by a ditch and a bank topped with a palisade. The motte might be a natural hill or outcrop, or it might be a manmade mound; it was usually linked to the bailey by a wooden bridge. The bailey contained essential buildings such as stables, kitchens, chapel and hall.

Gradually timber and earthwork was replaced with stone – although in a few cases, for instance at Richmond in

Right: At Dover, the vast stone square keep built by Maurice the Engineer for Henry II after 1168 still dominates the castle.

Yorkshire and Ludlow in Shropshire, castles were built partly or mostly in stone from the start. We cannot draw up a neat linear progression of developments in castle architecture – for example, from timber to stone, or of changes in tower design – that applies in all cases. Castles were usually enlarged and improved in a piecemeal fashion, and often details of history or topography dictated the kind of solution found in a particular place to a particular need.

POSITIONS OF STRENGTH

Within days of victory at the Battle of Hastings, William the Conqueror's men had erected simple timber and earthwork castles at Pevensey, Hastings and Dover. Then, as the great Norman lords spread out to take control of lands granted them by the king, they raised castles where they settled. The castles enforced and consolidated the Norman. Within two decades the Normans had built 100 castles in England.

The Normans often built in positions of natural strength and on the remains of earlier fortifications. The early castle at Dover was raised within the boundaries of an Iron Age hill fort and

Below: The imposing gatehouse tower of Pembroke Castle, built in the 13th century by William Marshall, Earl of Pembroke.

the Anglo-Saxon fortified town that had grown up on the site. The same applies to the castle at Hastings, while at Pevensey the Norman castle was built on the site of a Roman fort called Anderida.

In cities and prominent towns, castles were often built just within the outline of the existing Roman city walls and alongside strategically important land or river routes. In London the Normans built their first fortification in the south-east corner of the city walls and alongside the Thames; at Rochester in Kent, they built a great castle again within the Roman town walls and at the point where the Roman road connecting London to Dover passes across the river Medway.

THE TOWER KEEP

When the summit of the motte was encased in stone, the result was what historians call the 'shell keep', which

often – as at Windsor Castle and Restormel in Cornwall – enclosed timber or stone buildings for the lord's use in an inner courtyard. Elsewhere the lord's stronghold was often in a great stone tower – called magna turris ('great tower') by contemporaries and the 'tower keep' by historians.

Some tower keeps were built in the late 11th century – for example, at London (the Tower of London) and Colchester in Essex. Then throughout the following century tower keeps were regularly added to castles.

The Tower of London and the imposing tower of Colchester Castle were both rectangular in shape, but are generally called 'square keeps' by historians. These great structures were probably erected principally as a statement of the invaders' power, in emulation of the great 10th-century palace at Rouen in Brittany, capital of the dukes of Normandy, rather than as defensive structures. Later castle builders experimented in the 12th century with different shapes to find the one best suited to defence.

USING THIS BOOK
Many of the houses described in this book changed over time as architects added new buildings to the original design or modernized old structures. Therefore, some great historic houses appear in several parts of the book.

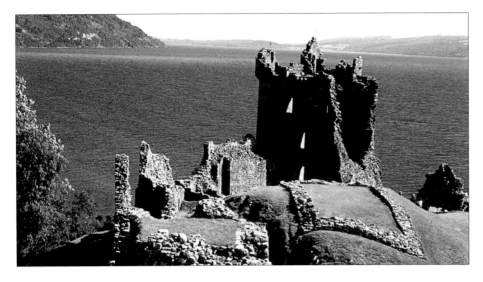

Above: Founded in the 13th century, the tower house of Castle Urquhart has unsurpassed views of Loch Ness.

At Orford in Suffolk King Henry II built a polygonal or many-sided tower in c.1173. The main tower was circular but it had three tall square turrets attached and a lower forebuilding containing the entrance. The design was an improvement on a square tower because it gave defenders a wider range of angles when firing arrows and other missiles at attackers. The polygonal design did not catch on, however; a more common shape was that of the cylindrical (circular) keep. Imposing

Below: Edward the Martyr was murdered at Corfe Castle in AD978. The castle controlled the gateway to the Isle of Purbeck.

12th-century examples survive even today at Conisbrough in Yorkshire, Pembroke in Wales and Dundrum in County Down, northern Ireland, among others. At Conisbrough Castle the circular tower has six square turret towers around it.

THE LAST REFUGE

The tower keep, like the palisaded motte in the early castles, formed an inner stronghold to which the lord and his bodyguard could retreat if the outer part of the castle were overrun by attackers. The lord's stronghold within the castle was called the 'dungeon' (from the Latin dominium via French donjon, meaning lordship). This word only acquired its modern meaning, of a dank and dark prison for the lord's enemies, in later times.

MURAL TOWERS AND GATEHOUSES

Stout towers were an important feature of the defensive walls built around the bailey. If they were projecting from the wall, they provided a strong position from which defenders could shoot at anyone trying to scale or undermine the outside of the wall. Because they rose higher than the wall, they were a raised shooting point from which defenders could attack people who had gained access to the top of the wall. At Dover, Maurice the Engineer, architect to King Henry II, greatly strengthened the Norman castle by building not only a great square stone keep but also a forbidding wall with ten rectangular towers in 1168–88.

The entrance was a particularly vulnerable point in such walls, and towers built above it or to either side of it resulted in the development of the castle gatehouse. Maurice's wall at Dover contained two heavily fortified gateways with twin towers. Such defences built out from the castle gateway, often in the form of a double tower, were called a barbican.

The gateway and barbican became a major feature, and in some castles such as Caerphilly and Beaumaris in Wales or Caerlaverock in Dumfries, Scotland, became perhaps the most secure part of the castle, containing some of its most prestigious apartments.

THE CONCENTRIC CASTLE

In the late 13th century the concentric castle – regarded by historians as the climax and perfection of British castle design – was developed in Wales, most notably at Caerphilly, built c.1271-80 by Gilbert de Clare, Lord of Glamorgan, and at Beaumaris, begun by Edward I in 1295. The concentric castle consisted of two rings of fortifications – an outer wall overlooked and protected by a taller and more heavily fortified inner wall.

This idea was as old as Ancient Egypt, but was essentially new to Britain. Edward and others had seen its effectiveness when on Crusade. In 1271-2 Edward, still a prince, had travelled on the Ninth Crusade to the Holy Land and had inspected and been greatly impressed by the concentric castle of Krak des Chevaliers, an originally Kurdish fortress in Syria that had been rebuilt by the chivalric brotherhood of the Knights Hospitaller. (On this same expedition he had visited Constantinople (now Istanbul), capital of the Byzantine empire, and been impressed by defensive walls raised in the 5th century by Emperor Theodosius II; Edward paid tribute to them in the castle he built at Caernarvon in north Wales in 1283.)

CASTLE AND FORTIFIED TOWN

Beaumaris Castle on Anglesey was the last of a series of great fortresses erected in north Wales by Edward I and his architect Master James of St Georges to celebrate and consolidate his conquest of the Welsh. As part of this programme, at Conway, Caernarvon and Flint Edward and Master James built castles alongside planned towns set within imposing defensive walls of their own. The castles were intended to hold a garrison of English soldiers and the walled towns were settled with English people to function both as a trading centre and a base for English administration of the territories beyond the walls. At Conway the town walls

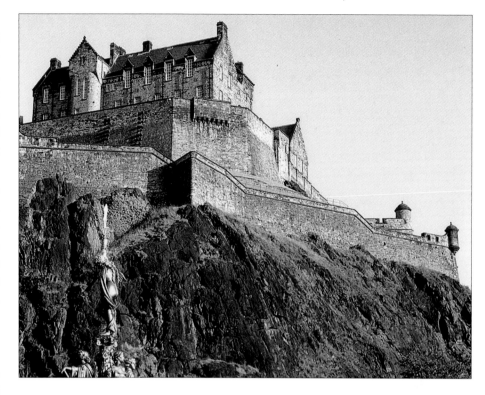

contained 21 towers and were as much as 24ft (7.5m) thick in places. The idea was based on that of the bastide, a similar settlement of fortress and walled town, which the English had built in Gascony, south-west France.

THE RISE OF THE FORTIFIED MANOR HOUSE

In early medieval warfare the possession of castles often provided the key to victory. King Stephen's long struggle against the Empress Matilda – through the '19 long winters' (1135–54) remembered by chroniclers – was

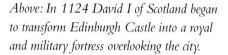

Above: In 1124 David I of Scotland began to transform Edinburgh Castle into a royal and military fortress overlooking the city.

conducted as a series of castle sieges. King John's battle against rebel lords in 1215 climaxed in a two-month siege of Rochester Castle. However, by the 15th century when the rival houses of York and Lancaster contested the throne in the Wars of the Roses, conflicts were decided not by siege but on the battlefield.

Lords still wanted battlements and gatehouses on their property – partly because a fortified house was prestigious, and partly because lawlessness had by no means been entirely eliminated – and so applied to the king for a 'licence to crenellate'. But increasingly they looked for comfort and luxury more than security in their homes. In properties such as Penshurst Place in Kent and Stokesay Castle in Shropshire, they achieved a level of fortification sufficient to deter passing marauders, but not to hold a besieging army at bay.

Left: The moat, towers and battlements at Bodiam Castle provide a perfect picture of what a medieval castle should be.

ENGLAND TIMELINE

Above: The Round Tower at Windsor Castle, Berkshire, was built in the 12th century.

Above: Middleham Castle, North Yorkhire, was the childhood home of Richard III.

Above: Bodiam Castle, East Sussex, is one of the finest examples of medieval building.

TO 1086

c.300BC At Maiden Castle in Dorset, Iron Age Britons begin building a vast hillfort. In AD43 the Roman army takes it from the Durotriges tribe.

c.AD75 Fishbourne Villa near Chichester, West Sussex, is a palace for King Cogidubnus of the Regnenses tribe.

c.AD250 At Porchester in Hampshire, the Romans build one of a series of 'Saxon shore forts'. Remains of other forts are at Richborough, Lympne and Pevensey.

c.AD850 Leede builds the original Leeds Castle in Kent.

1066 Duke William's army builds castles at Pevensey, Hastings, Dover, Canterbury, Wallingford, Berkhamsted and London.

1068 William the Conqueror founds castles at Warwick, Nottingham, York, Lincoln, Huntingdon and Cambridge.

c.1070 Alan Rufus, Earl of Yorkshire, builds Richmond Castle.

1072 William founds castles in Durham and at Bambrugh in Northumberland.

1075 William founds Windsor Castle.

c.1076 William orders the rebuilding in stone of the original earthwork castle in London. The White Tower at the Tower of London is complete by 1100.

c.1076 Norman monk Gundulf begins building Colchester Castle on the site of the Roman Temple of Claudius.

1085 Roger de Lacy builds Ludlow Castle in Shropshire.

1087–1299

1087-9 Rochester Castle, originally built of earth and stone, is rebuilt in stone by Bishop Gundulf of Rochester.

1097 King William Rufus begins building Westminster Hall on the site of King Edward the Confessor's palace.

c.1100 Roger de Bigod builds Framlingham Castle in Suffolk.

c.1140 Aubrey de Vere III, Earl of Oxford, builds Castle Hedingham in Essex.

1145 Reginald, an illegitimate son of Henry I, builds a castle on the site of an Iron Age Celtic fortress and Saxon fort at Tintagel in north Cornwall.

c.1150 Robert Fitz-Ranulph builds Middleham Castle in North Yorkshire.

1153 Robert Fitz-Harding, 1st Lord Berkeley, builds Berkeley Castle in Gloucestershire.

1165 Henry II builds the polygonal keep at Orford Castle in Suffolk.

1180 Hamelin de Plantagenet builds a cylindrical keep at Conisbrough Castle in South Yorkshire.

c.1250 Henry III makes lavish improvements to Westminster Palace, creating the superb King's Great Chamber.

1280 William de Valence, uncle of King Edward I, begins rebuilding Goodrich Castle in Hereford and Worcestershire.

1290 Wool merchant Lawrence of Ludlow fortifies his fine manor house of Stokesay Castle in Shropshire.

1300–1485

1300 Sir John de Broughton builds Broughton Castle near Banbury, Oxfordshire.

1302 A fire destroys much of the royal palace at Winchester, but the Great Hall survives.

c.1340 Sir John de Poulteney begins major rebuilding at Penshurst Place in Kent; Thomas, 3rd Lord Berkeley, builds the superb Great Hall at Berkeley Castle in Gloucestershire; Sir Thomas Cawne builds the Great Hall in the moated manor house of Ightham Mote, near Sevenoaks, Kent.

1370 The magnificent Banqueting Hall is built at Haddon Hall, Derbyshire.

c.1375 The Neville family builds Raby Castle in County Durham.

1385 Sir Edward Dakygrigge begins building Bodiam Castle in East Sussex.

1432 Sir John Falstaff begins building Caister Castle in Norfolk and Ralph, Lord Cromwell, builds his Great Tower at Tattershall Castle in Lincolnshire.

1441 Sir Roger de Fiennes begins building the fine fortified manor house of Herstmonceux Castle in East Sussex.

1477 King Edward IV begins building St George's Chapel at Windsor Castle.

c.1480 Edward IV builds a splendid Great Hall at Eltham Palace in Kent.

1482 Sir Edward Bedingfeld begins building the fortified manor house of Oxburgh Hall, near King's Lynn, Norfolk.

N
W **E**
S

SCOTLAND

Chesters
Roman Fort

Housesteads
Roman Fort

North Sea

Raby
Castle

Richmond
Castle

Middleham
Castle

Norton
Conyers

Irish Sea

ENGLAND

Peveril
Castle

Tattershall
Castle

Haddon
Hall

The Wash

Belvoir
Castle

Oxburgh
Hall

Caister
Castle

Stokesay
Castle

Framlingham
Castle

Warwick
Castle

Orford Castle

Ludlow
Castle

Sudeley
Castle

Broughton
Castle

Castle
Hedingham

WALES

Goodrich
Castle

Layer Marney
Tower

Berkhamsted
Castle

Tower of
London

Colchester Castle

Palace of Westminster
& Jewel Tower

Lullingstone
Roman
Villa

Rochester Castle

Berkeley
Castle

Windsor Castle

The Vyne

Hever
Castle

Ightham
Mote

Leeds
Castle

Dover
Castle

Bristol Channel

Winchester Castle
Great Hall

Penshurst Place

Great Dixter House

Strait of
Dover

Bignor Roman Villa

Maiden Castle

Porchester Castle

Lewes
Castle

Camber
Castle

Tintagel
Castle

Launceston
Castle

Fishbourne
Roman Palace

Herstmonceux
Castle

Pevensey
Castle

Hastings
Castle

English Channel

SCOTLAND, WALES
AND NORTHERN IRELAND TIMELINES

Above: Edinburgh Castle houses the Scottish Crown Jewels and the Stone of Destiny.

SCOTLAND, TO 1485

 1093 Queen (later Saint) Margaret of Scots builds a chapel in Edinburgh Castle. St Margaret's Chapel is the oldest surviving part of the castle.

1204 Alan, 2nd High Steward, begins work on Rothesay Castle, Isle of Bute.

1279 Unknown builders begin the unusual triangular castle of Caerlaverock in Dumfriesshire.

1296 William Wallace captures Dunnottar Castle, Aberdeenshire.

1300 King Edward I repairs Hermitage Castle, Borders, during the Scottish Wars of Independence.

1368-72 The future Robert II of Scots builds the 60ft(18m)-high David's Tower at Edinburgh Castle, the first known example in Scotland of the tower house.

1375 1st Earl of Douglas begins building Tantallon Castle, East Lothian, on a rocky promontory opposite the Bass Rock.

1424 King James I of Scots begins rebuilding Linlithgow Palace in West Lothian.

*c.*1435 King James I of Scots builds a Great Chamber at Edinburgh Castle.

*c.*1440 The main tower is added to Glamis Castle, Angus.

1460 Robert, 2nd Lord Maxwell, completes the building of Caerlaverock Castle, Dumfries & Galloway.

Irish Sea

Conway Castle
Flint Castle
Beaumaris Castle
Rhuddlan Castle
Caernarfon Castle
Criccieth Castle
Chirk Castle
Ruthin Castle
Harlech Castle
Powis Castle

Cardigan Bay

ENGLAND

WALES

Cilgerran Castle
Carreg Cennen Castle
Carmarthen Castle
Pembroke Castle
Kidwelly Castle
Raglan Castle
Abergavenny Castle
Chepstow Castle
Caerphilly Castle
Caerleon Roman Fort

Bristol Channel

Above: Beaumaris Castle, Wales, is the most technically perfect medieval castle in Britain.

WALES, TO 1485

1067 Chepstow Castle built.
1090 Abergavenny Castle built.
1106 Kidwelly Castle begun.
*c.*1200 Pembroke Castle begun.
1271 Caerphilly Castle begun.
1277 Edward I begins building Flint and Rhuddlan Castles, Denbighshire.
1283 Edward I begins building Conway, Caernarvon and Harlech castles.
1295 Edward I begins Beaumaris Castle.
1430 Sir William ap Thomas builds the Yellow Tower at Raglan Castle.

Above: Carrickfergus Castle, Northern Ireland, is dominated by its great keep.

NORTHERN IRELAND, TO 1485

*c.*1177 John de Courcy builds Dundrum Castle on the site of a Celtic hillfort overlooking Dundrum Bay.
*c.*1180 De Courcy builds Carrickfergus Castle overlooking Belfast Lough.
*c.*1180 De Courcy builds Killyleagh Castle to protect the inhabitants from Viking invaders.
1200s Building of Dunluce Castle begins.
1300s Building of Ardglass Castle begins.

Dunluce Castle
North Channel
NORTHERN IRELAND
Carrickfergus Castle
Killyleagh Castle
Ardglass Castle
Dundrum Castle
IRELAND
Irish Sea

THE MONARCHS

This list of monarchs names the kings and queens of Britain from the time of the ancient rulers of England and Scotland to the present day.

Much of the monarchy's authority and prestige derives from its ancient roots, from the centuries of historical continuity celebrated in genealogical and dynastic tables. Yet there are countless examples of force of arms and political manoeuvring intervening in dynastic or designated succession. In 1066, Duke William of Normandy famously had to enforce his claim that he was the designated successor of King Edward the Confessor in the face of several rival claims, including that of Harold Godwine, Earl of Wessex, who had himself declared King Harold II and was crowned on the very day after Edward the Confessor's death. William's claim triumphed at the Battle of Hastings.

The great Scottish national hero Robert the Bruce killed his chief rival to the succession, John Comyn, before having himself crowned King Robert I of Scots. Richard III of England occupied the throne at the expense of his uncrowned nephew, the 12-year-old King Edward V, whom Richard almost certainly had murdered in the Tower of London. King Henry VII won the English crown in battle against King Richard III.

Throughout these and many other upheavals, the theory of dynastic succession with God's blessing was maintained and all these kings – usurpers or murderers as they might be – laid claim to a dynastic link and were anointed as God's chosen servants on the throne. Henry IV, a usurper, brought an innovation to the coronation in an attempt to legitimize his rule. His ordination was the first to use holy oil reputedly given to Saint Thomas à Becket by the Virgin Mary.

KINGS AND QUEENS OF SCOTLAND (TO 1603)

THE HOUSE OF MACALPINE
Kenneth I mac Alpin 841–859
Donald I 859–863
Constantine I 863–877
Aed Whitefoot 877–878
Eochaid 878–889 (joint)
Giric 878–889
Donald II Dasachtach 889–900
Constantine II 900–943
Malcolm I 943–954
Indulf 954–962
Dubh 962–967
Culen 967–971
Kenneth II 971–995
Constantine III 995–997
Kenneth III 997–1005
Malcolm II 1005–1034

THE HOUSE OF DUNKELD
Duncan I 1034–1040
Macbeth 1040–1057
Lulach 1057–1058
Malcolm III Canmore 1058–1093
Donald III 1093–1094
Duncan II 1094
Donald III 1094–1097 (joint)

Above: James IV of Scotland presenting arms to his wife Queen Margaret, daughter of King Henry VII of England.

Edmund 1094–1097 (joint)
Edgar 1097–1107
Alexander I 1107–1124
David I 1124–1153
Malcolm IV the Maiden 1153–1165
William I the Lion 1165–1214
Alexander II 1214–1249
Alexander III 1249–1286
Margaret, Maid of Norway 1286–1290

THE HOUSE OF BALLIOL
John Balliol 1292–1296

THE HOUSE OF BRUCE
Robert I the Bruce 1306–1329
David II 1329–1332, 1338–1371

THE HOUSE OF BALLIOL
Edward Balliol 1332–1336

THE HOUSE OF STEWART
Robert II 1371–1390
Robert III 1390–1406
James I 1406–1437
James II 1437–1460
James III 1460–1488
James IV 1488–1513
James V 1513–1542
Mary, Queen of Scots 1542–1567
James VI 1567–1603

Below: King David II of Scotland (left) makes peace with King Edward III of England, in 1357.

KINGS AND QUEENS OF ENGLAND

THE HOUSE OF WESSEX
Egbert (802–839)
Aethelwulf (839–858)
Aethelbald (858–860)
Aethelbert (860–865/6)
Aethelred I (865/6–871)
Alfred the Great (871–899)
Edward the Elder (899–924/5)
Athelstan (924/5–939)
Edmund I (939–946)
Eadred (946–955)
Eadwig (955–959)
Edgar (959–975)
Edward the Martyr (975–978)
Aethelred II the Unready (978–1013,
    1014–1016)
Edmund Ironside (1016)

*Above: King John goes riding. Hunting
was the sport of kings from William I.*

THE DANISH LINE
Cnut (1016–1035)
Harald I Hardrada (1035–1040)
Harthacnut (1040–1042)

THE HOUSE OF WESSEX, RESTORED
Edward the Confessor (1042–1066)
Harold II (1066)

THE NORMANS
William I the Conqueror (1066–1087)
William II Rufus (1087–1100)
Henry I (1100–1135)
Stephen (1135–1154)

THE PLANTAGENETS
Henry II (1154–1189)
Richard I the Lionheart (1189–1199)
John (1199–1216)
Henry III (1216–1272)
Edward I (1272–1307)
Edward II (1307–1327)
Edward III (1327–1377)
Richard II (1377–1399)

THE HOUSE OF LANCASTER
Henry IV (1399–1413)
Henry V (1413–1422)
Henry VI (1422–1461, 1470–1471)

THE HOUSE OF YORK
Edward IV (1461–1470, 1471–1483)
Edward V (1483)
Richard III (1483–1485)

THE HOUSE OF TUDOR
Henry VII (1485–1509)
Henry VIII (1509–1547)
Edward VI (1547–1553)
Lady Jane Grey (1553)
Mary I (1553–1558)
Elizabeth I (1558–1603)

*Left: The heraldic badges of Kings
Edward III, Richard II and Henry IV
from Writhe's Garter Book.*

KINGS AND QUEENS OF GREAT BRITAIN

THE HOUSE OF STUART
James I (1603-1625)
Charles I (1625-1649)
Charles II (1660-1685)
James II (1685-1688)
William III and Mary II
    (1689-1694)
William III (1689-1702)
Anne (1702-1714)

THE HOUSE OF HANOVER
George I (1714-1727)
George II (1727-1760)
George III (1760-1820)
George IV (1820-1830)
William IV (1830-1837)
Victoria (1837-1901)

THE HOUSE OF SAXE-COBURG-GOTHA
Edward VII (1901-1910)

THE HOUSE OF WINDSOR
George V (1910-1936)
Edward VIII (1936)
George VI (1936-1952)
Elizabeth II (1952-)

*Below: The Archbishop of Canterbury
reverently places the crown on George V's
head at the coronation in 1911.*

CHAPTER ONE

FROM ROMAN VILLAS TO NORMAN CASTLES

TO 1154

Few buildings and fortifications remain of those that were constructed before the Norman followers of William the Conqueror invaded England in 1066. Wood and other biodegradable building materials have decayed, and what stone structures there were have generally been dismantled or incorporated into later buildings. With a few exceptions, we cannot visit pre-Norman buildings. However, there are extensive archaeological remains from which we can get an idea of the houses, palaces and fortresses built by native Britons, Romans and Anglo-Saxons.

Chronicle accounts of the dramatic events of 1066 repeatedly make plain the Normans' reliance upon the castle as both a military base and a means of overawing the people they came to conquer. Upon landing at Pevensey, Duke William of Normandy built a castle amid the remains of the Roman fort there, and at Hastings he raised another. At Dover, within days of the Battle of Hastings, he built a further castle, then at Canterbury yet another. Before the year was out, he had even erected a fortification at the south-east corner of the city wall of London itself.

By 1100, the Normans had built 400 castles in England. Each of the major Saxon towns had its Norman castle, and the borders were securely guarded by fortresses. Most comprised earthwork fortifications and timbers, and they were gradually rebuilt in stone in the late 11th and 12th centuries. Indeed, before the end of William I's reign in 1087, the first castles made entirely of stone were being built.

Left: The imposing Norman White Tower at the Tower of London was begun in 1078, using stone specially imported from Willliam the Conqueror's homeland in France.

BEFORE THE NORMANS
ROMAN AND ANGLO-SAXON BUILDING

 The ancient Romans' version of the country house or palace was the summer villa, an elegant building often lavishly decorated with murals and mosaics and equipped with the latest comforts, such as underfloor heating, and set in a well-tended estate. During the Roman occupation of Britain, villas were considered to be a status symbol both for the Romans and for the richest and most prominent of their subjects – as is still evident from the impressive remains of those buildings that have been excavated.

ROMAN VILLAS
At Fishbourne, near Chichester in West Sussex, are the remnants of a magnificent villa built c.AD75 for King Cogidubnus (or Togidubnus) of the Regnenses tribe. Archaeologists have determined that the villa had four wings arranged around a central courtyard, with a large reception chamber in the west wing. As many as 100 rooms at Fishbourne had mosaic floors, of which 20 survive, including a beautiful one representing the Roman love god Cupid riding a dolphin.

Below: The broch of Gurness, a fort on Orkney, is around 65ft (20m) across and was probably in use until around AD100.

Fishbourne was probably the grandest villa in the whole of Britain, and it was so large that it bears comparison with imperial villas in Italy. Other less magnificent but still remarkable Roman villas in Britain include Bignor near Arundel in West Sussex, Chedworth in Gloucestershire and also Lullingstone in Kent.

ANGLO-SAXON PALACES
There are also a few tantalizing remains of the palaces and grand houses built by Anglo-Saxon kings in the years after the

Above: The ancient British fort of Maiden Castle, Dorset, covers 45 acres (18ha). Vespasian's forces captured it in AD43.

Roman withdrawal from Britain. The kings of Northumbria, for example, built a palace complex on raised ground at Yeavering in Northumberland in the 7th–9th centuries AD. The most important building of the complex, the Great Hall, was built entirely of wood and had a great central hearth and entrances in the long sides of the building. Roof posts were erected in pairs down the length of the building, which had the effect of dividing the space into three separate aisles.

Archaeologists have uncovered what may be the remains of palaces kept by the great King Offa of Mercia at Sutton in Herefordshire and on the banks of the River Thames at Chelsea in London. Another great Anglo-Saxon hall that may have been a palace was found at Northampton; while at Cheddar in Somerset, a building once thought to be a palace is more likely to have been a less grand building, perhaps a hunting lodge.

FORTS AND FORTRESSES

The remains of more than 2,500 hilltop fortresses built by ancient Britons have been identified. Most are small, and offered protection to just a few peasants and their cattle, but the remnants of very extensive hilltop fortresses from the 1st millennium BC can be seen at Maiden Castle in Dorset, Hengistbury Head in Hampshire and Old Sarum in Wiltshire.

In northern Scotland and on Orkney and the Shetland Isles, locals seeking protection against raiders built fortified round towers, or brochs, at about this time. The Broch of Gurness on Orkney is 65ft (20m) across and once stood 32ft (10m) tall; Mousa Broch, on the isle of Mousa off Shetland, still stands 42ft (13m) tall and is 50ft (15m) in diameter.

When the Romans conquered Britain, they very rarely used the existing British fortifications as strongholds, preferring to build their own fortresses. Some of these Roman forts have been excavated, giving an indication of their size and importance. Caerleon in Monmouthshire was a 50-acre (20-ha) fort. Its wall had defensive turrets every 150ft (46m) and the fortress had an amphitheatre for both military manoeuvres and entertainment.

At the northern limit of their empire, the Romans built Hadrian's Wall, which ran for 73 miles (117km) from

Below: The Roman camp at Caerleon was one of three permanent legionary forts in Britain in the late 1st century AD.

Newcastle to Carlisle. After every mile (1.6km), soldiers built a small 'Mile Castle' fortification, and after every 4 miles (6.5km), they erected a garrison fort, such as the one at Housesteads in Northumberland, which was built c.AD124 and has been fully excavated. It had room to garrison up to 1,000 men.

In south-east England are the remnants of Roman coastal fortifications, the Saxon shore forts, built to repel a possible sea-borne invasion. The most complete remains are at Portchester Castle in Hampshire. The 9-acre (3.6-ha) fort had walls 20ft (6m) high and 10ft (3m) thick, with D-shaped towers every 100–200ft (30–60m), from which defenders would have fired catapults. Large parts are still standing.

Anglo-Saxon kings needed to fortify their palace settlements against Viking raiders. King Alfred (r.871–99), for instance, garrisoned a series of forts for this purpose throughout his kingdom of Wessex, remains of which can be seen.

Many Roman and Anglo-Saxon forts later formed the basis of Norman stone castles: including the Roman fortresses at Pevensey, Porchester, Caerleon and Caerphilly. Excavations at Goltho, Lincolnshire, reveal how an Anglo-Saxon hall-palace complex was given ditch and bank defences in AD850–1000 and then was the site of a Norman motte-and-bailey castle in 1080–1150.

Above: This mosaic from the Roman villa at Lullingstone, Kent, shows the god Jupiter (in the form of a bull) carrying off Europa.

Below: King Alfred the Great – for whom this fine jewelled bookmark head was made – established around 30 fortified burghs (boroughs) to keep the Vikings at bay.

PEVENSEY AND HASTINGS
THE FIRST CASTLES

Along with Hastings, Dover and Canterbury, Pevensey Castle was among the first four Norman castles built in England. Duke William of Normandy began to build a castle at Pevensey within the west gate of the Roman fort there, on the very first day of the Conquest campaign, 28 September 1066. According to one chronicler, William's invasion force carried with it, packed in boxes, the materials needed for quickly raising a wooden tower and other defensive structures.

OCCUPATION OF ANDERIDA

The Roman fort of Anderida at Pevensey – later one of the Saxon shore line of fortresses – was sited on a peninsula overlooking the sea, for at the time of the Roman occupation, and indeed of the Norman Conquest, the waves came in as far as the castle walls, although the sea has now fallen back to leave marshland. In 1066, the fort was the site of an Anglo-Saxon burgh, or fortified town, and the remains of a chapel excavated within the castle walls are probably those of this burgh. William and his Norman forces encountered no resistance when they took control and hastily erected their castle.

ROBERT, COUNT OF MORTAIN

In the autumn of 1066, Duke William did not linger at Pevensey, but moved his army swiftly on to Hastings. After the Conquest, he gave Pevensey Castle and its lordship to his half-brother Robert, Count of Mortain. Robert was also made Lord of Berkhamsted, Lambeth and Bermondsey, and in 1072 of Cornwall. He was England's second-largest lay landowner, although he spent little time in the country, preferring to live in Normandy.

Above: Pevensey Castle in Sussex survived sieges by the forces of King William Rufus (1088) and Simon de Montfort (1264).

PEVENSEY CASTLE

Robert strengthened the existing walls of the Roman fort at Pevensey to form the outer bailey wall of the castle. He repaired the eastern gateway and built a new entrance to replace the ancient one at the south-west. He then erected a second walled enclosure within and at the eastern end of the ancient fort.

The castle's stone tower-keep was probably built after Robert's death (1095), in the early 1100s, when many of the wooden Conquest castles were rebuilt in stone. It made use of part of the Roman wall and a Roman tower. On the other three sides of the inner bailey (or enclosure), the walls and D-shaped towers were probably erected in the mid-1200s by Peter of Savoy, Earl of Richmond and uncle of Henry III's wife, Queen Eleanor. Henry made Peter Lord of Pevensey in 1246. Peter built residential apartments set against the inside of the castle walls in a very grand style befitting his status.

As the sea retreated, uncovering Pevensey Marshes, the castle declined in importance. By the Tudor period, it had begun to fall into ruins. Nevertheless, it was partially refortified as a gun emplacement in the 1580s to defend

---

MOTTE-AND-BAILEY CASTLES

The early Norman castles combined a motte (a mound) surrounded by a ditch and a bailey (an enclosed, defended area). The bailey was enclosed by a wooden fence, and outside that by another ditch or a moat. Sometimes the motte was a hill; at other times it was an artificial mound built up using the earth that had been dug out when the ditch was made.

On the motte stood a keep (a look-out tower), in the early years also made of wood. It often contained accommodation for the castellan (keeper of the castle). Within the bailey were the buildings necessary to house and maintain the garrison – perhaps a Great Hall, kitchens, chapel, stables and other farm buildings.

Right: At Launceston, Cornwall, a timber keep was built on a steep motte c.1067. The stone castle is late 12th century.

In the late 11th–12th century, the wooden keep was often rebuilt in stone. The outer wall around the bailey was also remade in stone, with the addition of a strong 'gatehouse' and a drawbridge across the moat.

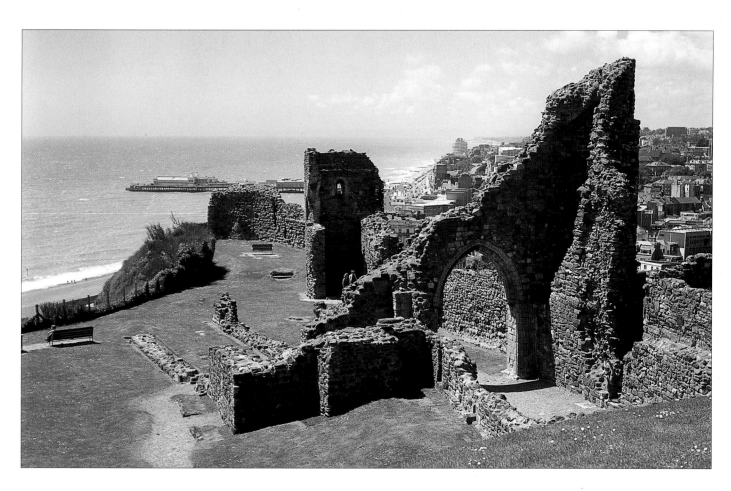

Above: The original timber motte-and-bailey castle of 1066 at Hastings, Sussex, was rebuilt in stone as early as 1070.

against a Spanish invasion. Almost 400 years later, it housed military billets and machine-gun posts during World War II.

HASTINGS CASTLE

An image in the Bayeux Tapestry shows William's men digging to create a ditch and raise a motte at Hastings. As he would later do at Dover, he built the motte of his castle within the outline of an Iron Age hill fortress and an Anglo-Saxon burgh, and close to a pre-existing church, which is now known as St-Mary-in-the-Castle. The castle occupied a commanding position on a coastal hill-top overlooking the beach and harbour. A tower was added in the 12th century; an eastern curtain wall (with a twin-

Right: At Hastings, William, then Duke of Normandy, supervises his men digging out a ditch and using the earth to build a motte, in this scene from the Bayeux Tapestry.

towered gatehouse) and the South Tower were built in the 13th century. Later the cliff was so severely eroded by the sea that parts of the castle fell into it.

After victory at Hastings, and building a castle at Dover, William marched in a circuitous route on London and erected castles *en route* at Canterbury in Kent, Wallingford in Oxfordshire (where Archbishop Stigand of Canterbury submitted to him) and Berkhamsted in Hertfordshire. Earthworks and other castle remains can still be seen in all these towns.

DOVER CASTLE
THE STONE KEEP

In October 1066, within days of victory at the Battle of Hastings, and after building Pevensey and Hastings Castles, William the Conqueror began to build his castle at Dover. He set to work inside the boundaries of an Iron Age hillfort that had been adapted by the Romans and then become a fortified town. The pre-Norman church of St Mary-in-Castro, dating from the late 10th or early 11th century, survives within the castle precincts – alongside a Roman *pharos*, or lighthouse. The earth bank and ditch outside the castle's later 12th-century walls are probably the remains of the fortifications that were established on the site by its Iron Age colonizers.

According to the account of William of Poitiers, the first Norman castle at Dover was built in just eight days. Presumably, it was an earthwork and wooden motte-and-bailey fortification. This would have been quite a feat, as

Below: English stronghold. Constables of Dover Castle have included Henry V and Henry VIII (while princes), the Duke of Wellington and Sir Winston Churchill.

motte construction was very labour intensive, and the soldiers needed to be on constant guard. All that remains today is a stretch of the ditch and bank alongside the south transept of the church. King William made his half-brother Bishop Odo of Bayeux the first constable of the castle at Dover.

THE STONE KEEP
William's castle at Dover was greatly strengthened by Henry II (r.1154–89) and his architect Maurice the Engineer in 1168–88. Maurice built the vast square stone keep, or tower, which is the dominant building in the castle complex

Left: Henry II, who built the great keep at Dover, brought stability to England after the civil war of King Stephen's reign.

to this day. Measuring 96 x 96 x 98ft (29 x 29 x 30m), with walls 16–21ft (5–6.5m) thick, this massive rectangular stone keep was the largest in Europe. It contained four great rooms measuring 20 x 50ft (6 x 15m), and two chapels, in addition to a further 12 rooms, each roughly 10 x 15ft (3 x 4.5m), within the extremely thick walls.

THE CASTLE WALLS
Maurice also raised the inner bailey wall at Dover, complete with ten rectangular towers, and two twin-tower gateways with barbicans (outer fortifications defending a drawbridge or gateway) – one to the north (the King's Gate) and one to the south (the Palace Gate). Furthermore, Henry and Maurice began work on an outer curtain wall, in this way anticipating the principles of the concentric castle design, with its twin defensive walls, around 100 years ahead of the design's more general application in the reign of Edward I.

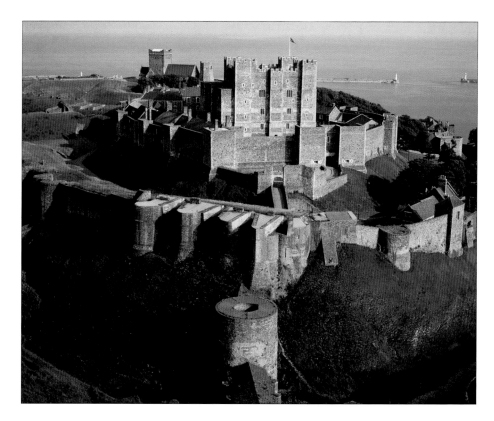

Above: The castle at Dover with (beyond, left) the Church of St Mary-in-Castro and the Roman lighthouse.

NORMAN RINGWORKS

In addition to motte-and-bailey castles, the Normans built fortifications known as 'ringworks' – defensive strongholds enclosed by earthworks but without a motte. These were sometimes quite small, less than 30m (100ft) across within the earthworks, but in other places they were of considerable size: a ringwork excavated at Huttons Ambo in Yorkshire measured 120 x 180ft (35 x 55m) within its bank and ditch defences.

Historians emphasize that the castle was a symbol of high status within the rigidly hierarchical feudal system, adding that ringworks may have been built for landowners who did not have sufficient feudal standing to justify a motte and a castle. Another explanation is that ringworks were preferred in places where a large garrison force was needed, since the castle and motte fortification could leave little room to house defenders.

The outer wall of the castle was completed by King John (r.1199–1216). At the close of John's reign, when the king was in open conflict with many of his barons, the castle was besieged by Prince Louis of France, who had been invited by the barons to invade. Despite the great expenditure on its walls by King Henry II, and a determined defence by constable Hubert de Burgh, the castle came close to being captured when Louis of France and his engineers succeeded in undermining the King's Gate, part of which collapsed. However, King John's death brought the conflict to an end before matters could get worse.

Henry III (r.1216–72) carried out extensive improvements at Dover Castle. Most notable was the erection of the Norfolk Towers in place of the former King's Gate and the addition of the Constable's Gate, containing residential quarters for the castellan or keeper of the castle, c.1227.

LATER YEARS

Dover Castle's position ensured that it remained an important element of England's maritime defences across the centuries. Many later alterations were made that, sadly, damaged the remains of the medieval castle. These included knocking down towers in the outer wall to establish gun emplacements during the Napoleonic War, when an extensive network of tunnels was first dug into the cliff beneath the castle. In World War II, Operation Dynamo (the May 1940 evacuation of 338,000 British soldiers from Dunkirk, northern France) was masterminded by 700 top-secret staff from the tunnels. Within the tunnels there was a hospital as well as a command centre that Churchill visited to see the plans that led to eventual victory.

Below: An early concentric castle in England? This reconstruction of Dover Castle in the mid-1300s shows inner and outer defences.

THE TOWER OF LONDON
AND WILLIAM I

Six weeks after their triumph at Hastings, the Normans marched into London from the north-west, following a route from the battlefield via Dover, Canterbury, Winchester, Wallingford and Berkhamsted. The main aim of this long march was to make an impressive show of military force and to cow the population into submission. William sent an advance party into London to build a castle there, and, after his coronation on 25 December 1066, he retreated to Barking until it was finished.

The first London fortification was built in the south-east corner of the city's Roman walls. With the River Thames to the south and the city walls also to the south and to the east, the castle-builders built trenches and an

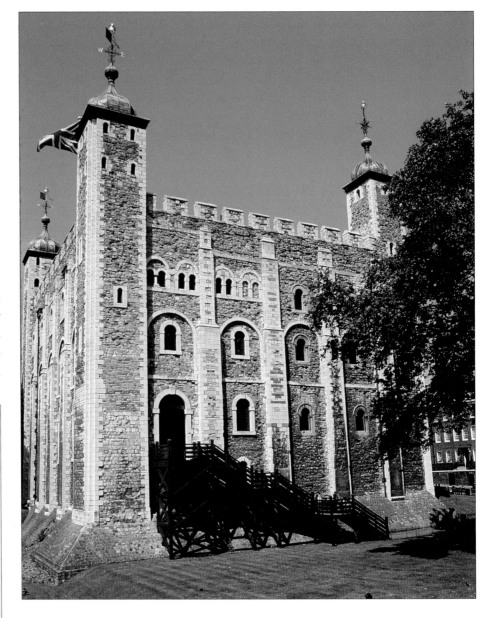

Above: The Tower of London was already being used as a prison by 1100, when Bishop Flambard of Durham escaped through a high window using a rope.

earthwork wall with a wooden palisade to the north and west. The trenches were 25ft (8m) wide and 11ft (3.5m) deep.

THE WHITE TOWER

Around a decade later, in 1078, William ordered the building of a great square stone keep, the White Tower, which was intended to strike fear into the hearts of any subversive Londoners. This vast and forbidding building, which survives to this day (see also page 102), was largely complete by *c.*1100. The tower, 90ft (27m) high with walls 11–15ft (3.5–4.5m) thick, measured 105 x 118ft (32 x 36m).

It contained a basement beneath two floors of residential apartments, both containing a hall, chamber and chapel. The top floor was set aside for the king himself. The tower's sole entrance was on the south side, some 15ft (4.5m) above ground and accessed by steps that could be removed. The White Tower was probably designed by Gundulf, a Norman monk who became Bishop of Rochester.

THE SQUARE KEEP

The rectangular tower of Colchester Castle and the White Tower of London are the earliest examples of the square keep in England. The former, at 107 x 151ft (32.5 x 46m), was larger even than the White Tower. These towers may have been based on the design of the ducal palace at Rouen of *c.*950. They were intended more as an expression of the might of the Norman invaders than as military strongholds.

Below: The vast Norman keep at Colchester was built over the vaults of the ruined Roman Temple of Claudius.

WESTMINSTER HALL
HEART OF THE PALACE

 When William the Conqueror was satisfied with the fortifications he had built in the city of London, he moved his court into King Edward the Confessor's palace at Westminster. Edward had built this in 1060 on ground between the River Thames and the abbey church of Westminster (subsequently Westminster Abbey).

KING WILLIAM RUFUS

William the Conqueror's son, William Rufus, had grand plans to build a new palace on the site, and in 1097 he built the first stage: Westminster Hall. His structure is the only part of the 11th-century palace still standing today, since it survived the fire that devastated the ancient buildings in 1834.

William Rufus's hall was used for banquets. It measured a massive 240ft (73m) in length and was almost 40ft (12m) high, with walls 6ft 8in (2m) thick.

Below: King George IV's lavish Coronation Banquet was held in Westminster Hall, in 1821. The Earl of Denbigh wrote of the event that 'it exceeded all imagination'.

A raised gallery ran around the hall 20ft (6m) above the ground. The walls were plastered and painted, and contained round-headed windows. The roof was supported by great timber posts, which divided the vast room into a central nave and two side aisles. Although William was reputedly not very impressed with the new building – declaring it a 'mere bedchamber' – he held a great banquet in 1099 to celebrate its completion. The Royal Council of bishops, nobles and ministers, which later assembled there, was the forerunner of the present House of Lords.

Above: This engraving by Wenceslaus Holler shows Westminster Hall (centre) as it appeared in the English Civil War.

AFFAIRS OF STATE

The hall's appearance has significantly changed since King William Rufus's day. After it was damaged by fire in 1291, Edward II carried out restoration; in addition, Richard II made several major improvements in 1397–9, including installing a vast hammer-beam roof (see page 70). Later, the hall was the setting for the coronation feast of each new monarch, when, following tradition, the king or queen's champion would ride to the centre of the hall and challenge to single combat anyone who opposed the sovereign's right to rule. The last coronation feast held in the hall was for George IV in 1821, which was, like all his entertainments, incredibly lavish.

The hall has also been the setting for a number of important trials, including those of Sir Thomas More in 1535, the Gunpowder Plot conspirators in 1606 and King Charles I in 1649. Its main everyday function is as the vestibule of the House of Commons. Since the death of Queen Victoria, it has also been used for the lying-in-state of deceased royals, such as Edward VII (1910), George VI (1952) and Queen Elizabeth, the Queen Mother (2002).

CHEPSTOW CASTLE
NORMAN BUILDING IN WALES

William FitzOsbern was the childhood friend of William the Conqueror and veteran of the Battle of Hastings. He began work on a stone castle at Chepstow in south-east Wales in 1067. Created Earl of Hereford, FitzOsbern established Chepstow as a base for Norman penetration into Wales. It was built in stone from the beginning.

The castle was built in a strategic position – a long, high cliff overlooking the River Wye and the place where the Roman road from western England into South Wales forded the river. Its principal building was a stone Great Hall, initially of two storeys; this was altered and raised in the 13th century, but its original walls are still standing, making it Britain's oldest surviving stone castle building. FitzOsbern and his masons used bands of red tiles thought to be from the nearby Roman fort of Caerwent; they also inserted Norman round-headed windows on the ground floor, which can still be seen today. There are also surviving sections of the 11th-century stone defensive walls to the east (now in the middle bailey) and west (now in the upper bailey).

FitzOsbern's castle was largely complete by 1071, when the Earl was killed in battle in Flanders. By then he had made good use of his base to stamp his authority on much of the Welsh

THE NORMANS IN WALES

Chepstow was the earliest of several castles erected on the borders of Wales (the Marches) by the Norman 'Marcher lords', who took an iron grip on the English-Welsh border. (The term 'Marcher' derives from the Frankish *marka*, meaning 'boundary'.) Just as William FitzOsbern was given the earldom of Hereford and built a castle at Chepstow, so Roger of Montgomery was created Earl of Shrewsbury and raised a castle at Pembroke, South Wales, and Hugh de Avranches was made Earl of Chester and built a castle in that city. Many other Norman castles followed in Wales, including notable examples at Cardiff (built c.1091 by Robert Fitzhamon, Norman lord of Gloucester), Abergavenny (built c.1090 by Hamelin de Ballon), Kidwelly (built in the 12th century by Roger, Bishop of Salisbury) and Caerphilly (built from 1271 onward by Gilbert de Clare).

Below: Kidwelly Castle was rebuilt after c.1275 by Payn de Chaworth.

kingdom of Gwent. However, his son, Roger Fitzwilliam, lost possession of Chepstow when he joined the doomed uprising against the Conqueror in 1075. Roger was imprisoned, his castle and lands reverting to the Crown.

WILLIAM MARSHALL
In 1115, Henry I gave the castle to the powerful de Clare family, who seem to have made no notable alterations. Then, in 1189, the de Clare heiress, Isabel, daughter of Richard 'Strongbow' de Clare,

Left: Chepstow Castle's walls are 18ft (5.5m) thick in parts. They are notable for an early use of round and square towers.

Earl of Pembroke, married the great knight William Marshall, and the castle passed into his hands along with all her other estates. Marshall upgraded the defences at Chepstow significantly, rebuilding the eastern defensive wall and adding two projecting round towers with arrow slits through which archers could defend the land immediately outside the wall. (The curtain wall he raised was, in his day, the eastern boundary of the castle, but because of subsequent developments, it is now the dividing wall between the middle and lower baileys.)

In the years to 1245, William Marshall's sons continued to redevelop the castle, adding a further enclosure to the east (now the lower bailey) with a twin-towered gatehouse, and at the other, western, end of the castle building a barbican with a cylindrical tower. They also improved the Great Keep, adding large windows on the safer northern side overlooking the Wye.

ROGER BIGOD III

In 1270–1300 the castle was in the hands of another great landholder, Roger Bigod III, Earl of Norfolk. He built a new hall along the northern (cliff) side of the lower bailey, including a cellar, kitchen, service rooms and accommodation, as well as the public space of the hall. In addition, he erected what is now known as Marten's Tower, containing elegant accommodation for the lord of the castle and a richly decorated chapel, at the south-east angle of the lower bailey. Earl Roger also built a new three-storey gatehouse for the barbican, added an extra storey to William FitzOsbern's Great Keep and erected the town walls for the developing

Below: Interior of Marten's Tower, Chepstow. Henry Marten, who was jailed there, was a leader of the Levellers in the Civil War.

Above: River fortress. The Wye runs along the north edge of the escarpment on which the elongated castle stands at Chepstow.

settlement alongside the castle. The town of Chepstow grew in the 13th and 14th centuries and received a charter in 1524.

The castle was garrisoned for Charles I and came twice under siege during the Civil Wars of the 17th century. In forcing its surrender, parliamentary guns caused damage, but the castle was later repaired and garrisoned by both Cromwell and Charles II. Marten's Tower takes its name from Henry Marten, one of the judges who signed Charles I's death warrant and who, after the Restoration in 1660, was imprisoned with his wife (in some comfort) in the tower by Charles II. Marten died there in 1680.

ROCHESTER CASTLE
STRONGHOLD IN STONE

The original Rochester Castle was one of the earliest Norman fortifications, built shortly after the Conquest as a show of strength and to guard the point at which the Roman road from London to Dover crossed the River Medway in Kent. It was constructed of timber and earthworks in the south-west angle of the Roman city wall at the point where the medieval bridge spanned the river. In 1087–9, the first years of King William Rufus's reign, Bishop Gundulf – architect of the White Tower in London – rebuilt the castle walls in stone. Rochester was therefore one of the first Norman castles to be reworked in stone.

THE SQUARE KEEP

In 1127, King Henry I granted the castle to William de Corbeil, Archbishop of Canterbury, and his successors. The archbishop built a remarkable square keep, 70 x 70ft (21 x 21m), 113ft (34.5m) high to the parapet, with turrets at the corners soaring another 12ft (3.5m). The walls were 12ft (3.5m) thick at their base. The keep was forbidding

Below: A 19th-century painting of Rochester shows how close the cathedral stands to the castle, which guards the crossing of the River Medway.

Above: The square keep at Rochester Castle, showing the rounded south-east tower, rebuilt after damage in the siege of 1215.

without but luxurious within: the second floor housed a chapel, a Great Chamber and a Great Hall, with magnificent carving around the fireplaces, windows and doors, and a raised gallery to the hall. The keep also contained a defensive cross wall, behind which defenders could retreat if the tower was partially breached, and which came in

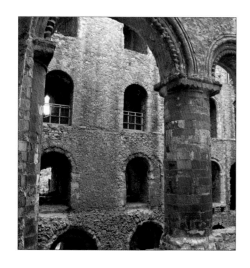

Above: The interior of the great keep of Rochester Castle is now little more than a shell, but the sheer size of the ruins gives a sense of its original luxury and grandeur.

useful for the castle defenders in 1215 (see below). A smaller tower, built against the north face of the keep, guarded the entrance, which was at first-floor level.

THE FIRST SIEGE

Archbishop de Corbeil's square keep at Rochester faced two major sieges in its history. The first came in 1215, when, with many of England's leading barons openly opposing King John, the Archbishop of Canterbury, Stephen Langton, refused to open the castle to the pro-Royalist Bishop of Winchester. King John and his army arrived, and laid siege for around two months, held at bay by a garrison of little more than 100 men. The king's men used five stone-throwing engines, which did great damage to the curtain wall but could make no significant impact on the tremendous fortifications of the keep itself, so instead they set out to undermine the south-east angle of the tower. They dug beneath the corner of the building and shored up the brickwork with wooden props, then set fire to the props, causing part of the tower to collapse. The defenders retreated behind the defensive cross wall and continued the fight, but the garrison was reduced to surrender by starvation.

After the siege of 1215, the damaged south-east corner of the keep was restored in the contemporary style as a cylindrical (circular) turret, in contrast to the square turrets at the other corners of the tower. Other repairs and improvements included reconstruction of the castle's outer gate and the building of a drawbridge in the southern curtain wall.

In 1264, Rochester Castle was besieged by Simon de Montfort and other rebels during the baronial uprising against King Henry III. The castle was badly damaged, but withstood the assault for a week, until de Montfort and his men withdrew at the news that the King's army was on its way to relieve the castle.

LATER YEARS

In later years, the castle fell into disrepair, but it was restored and rebuilt in the 14th century by Kings Edward III and Richard II. Then it suffered many more years of neglect before being passed from the Crown to private owners in the reign of James I.

MARCHER FORTRESS: LUDLOW CASTLE

Ludlow Castle in Shropshire was built in 1085 as a Norman stronghold to subdue the 'Marches' (the English–Welsh border). Its first lord, Roger de Lacy, was granted land in south Shropshire by William FitzOsbern, Earl of Hereford and builder of Chepstow Castle. At Ludlow, using locally quarried stone, de Lacy built one of the great stone keeps of the 12th century, on high land overlooking the River Terne. The de Lacy family lost the castle for some years, during which, *c.*1130, Sir Joyce de Dinan built a remarkable circular chapel in the Middle Ward, but the castle subsequently returned to its original owners. The town of Ludlow was laid out in the 12th century to the east of the fortress.

In later years, Ludlow Castle belonged to Roger Mortimer, the ruthless Earl of March; his descendants probably built the fortifications on the castle's northern front. The castle then passed to Edward IV. Many improvements were made to the castle in the Tudor period, when it was briefly the home of Prince Arthur (elder brother of the eventual King Henry VIII) and his bride, Catherine of Aragon. In the tower named after Prince Arthur, the sickly heir to the throne died in 1502 – an event with momentous consequences for England's royal family.

Below: In Ludlow's inner bailey stands the Chapel of St Mary Magdalene – the only round 'church' in an English castle.

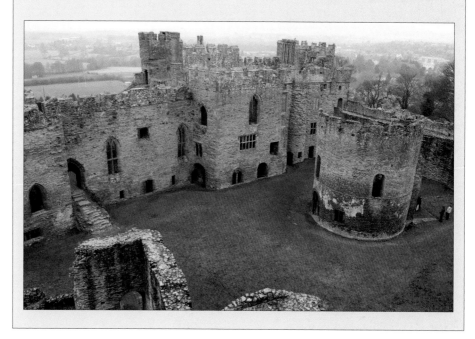

CASTLE HEDINGHAM
THE GREAT TOWER

Castle Hedingham in Essex is celebrated as one of the most splendid 12th-century rectangular keeps in England. The vast stone tower, 110ft (33.5m) high, was built *c*.1140 by Aubrey de Vere III, probably to celebrate his elevation to the earldom of Oxford.

TOWER CASTLE

The keep has four floors above a basement: the first contains the entrance chamber and the second and third floors combine to make the great Banqueting Hall. Around the hall, built into the 12ft (3.5m) thick walls, runs an elevated minstrels' gallery. The hall and gallery make Hedingham comparable to the Great Keep at Rochester, built perhaps a decade earlier.

Above: The 28ft (8.5m) transverse arch in the Banqueting Hall at Hedingham is one of the largest Norman arches in England.

Castle Hedingham once had four corner turrets and a forebuilding on the west face containing the first-floor entrance to the tower, again as at Rochester. But two of Hedingham's turrets and most of the forebuilding have now been demolished. In other respects, however, it survives in remarkably good condition, with floors and roof intact.

The keep stood in the inner bailey, separated from the outer bailey to the east by a ditch (now crossed by a Tudor bridge). Remains of a Great Hall and a chapel have been found in the inner bailey. The inner and outer bailey were enclosed by earthwork and ditch defences.

The castle remarkably remained in the de Vere family until 1703, on the death of the 20th Earl of Oxford.

Left: Only two of the original four corner turrets survive on the four-floor rectangular tower at Castle Hedingham.

BERKELEY CASTLE
THE ROUND KEEP

The first documented castle at Berkeley in Gloucestershire was built by Roger de Berkeley, as recorded in the Domesday Survey of 1086. Earlier, the land had belonged to Earl Godwin of Wessex, father of Harold II, and after Harold's defeat at Hastings was granted by the Conqueror to the immensely powerful William FitzOsbern, Earl of Hereford, builder of Chepstow Castle and holder of large swathes of land in western and south-western England. There were fortifications on the site before Roger de Berkeley's castle.

THE KEEP

The oldest surviving building at Berkeley is the magnificent round keep, completed in 1153 by Robert Fitz-Harding, 1st Lord Berkeley. Lord Robert received the estate from King Henry II, who had taken the castle from its previous lord, another Roger de Berkeley, following the lawlessness of King Stephen's reign. The keep stands 62ft (19m) high and is 90ft (27m) in diameter. Its walls

Below: Berkeley Castle's inner bailey, 1822. In one of the apartments are the ebony bed and chairs used by Sir Francis Drake on his round-the-world voyage of 1577–80.

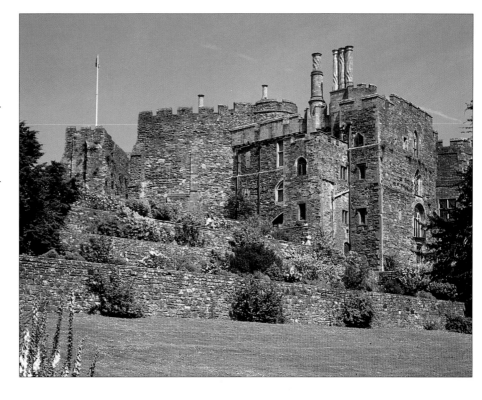

enclose the mound of the earlier motte-and-bailey Norman fortification, although rather than being placed on top of the motte, the tower here surrounds it. The entrance was by a staircase on the eastern side, enclosed in a forebuilding in the 14th century. The ascent was by 'trip steps', made deliberately in varying sizes so that attackers mounting in a hurry would be likely to lose their footing.

Above: Edward II was murdered at Berkeley in 1327. The Berkeley descendants of Robert Fitz-Harding still live at the castle.

The keep originally had four semi-circular turrets, all now gone. Two were incorporated into 14th-century buildings within the enclosure, one was replaced by a new gatehouse and the fourth by Thorpe Tower. The remodelling was carried out largely by Thomas, 3rd Lord Berkeley, in 1340–50, when he added the magnificent Great Hall in the castle's inner bailey (see page 68). This hall, 32ft tall and 62ft in length (10 x 19m), was raised on the site of the original hall. It is hung with fine tapestries and has beautiful stained glass windows.

LATER HISTORY

Berkeley Castle was besieged by a parliamentary army during the Civil War in 1645, when their guns made a breach measuring 35ft (11m) in the walls of the keep. This breach has never been repaired, remaining to this day as a reminder of the castle's past as a working fortress.

RICHMOND CASTLE
NORTHERN STRONGHOLDS

The Norman castle of Richmond in North Yorkshire dates to within a decade of the Conquest and occupies a commanding position on a spur overlooking the River Swale. It was built by Alan Rufus of Brittany, Earl of Yorkshire, who was given the vast lands of Edwin, the Saxon Earl of Mercia, as a reward for loyal service to William the Conqueror at Hastings. Richmond Castle was probably built after the Normans had decisively stamped their authority on northern England in the ruthless 'Harrying of the North' during the winter of 1069–70.

SCOLLAND'S HALL

The oldest surviving part of the castle is Scolland's Hall, a sizeable, very early stone two-storey keep built *c*.1071–5. The now-ruined building once contained a Great Hall on the first floor, as well as private apartments for the lord and a tower containing a garderobe, or area for dressing. Alan Rufus also

built a long curtain wall enclosing a large, roughly triangular bailey called the Great Court of around 2.5 acres (1ha), which takes its curious shape from that of the hilltop land it occupies. He fortified the south-west corner of the

Above: The two-storey building that survives in the corner of the triangular Great Court at Richmond is Scolland's Hall of c.1075.

enclosure with a rectangular defensive tower and added three more towers along the eastern stretch of the curtain wall. In the most northerly of these, Robin Hood's Tower, was a fine chapel dedicated to St Nicholas. This tower is also believed to have been the prison of King William 'the Lion' of Scots in 1174 after he was captured at Alnwick. Another chapel (now gone) appears from archaeological evidence to have stood in the western part of the Great Court. Beyond Scolland's Hall to the south was an outer defensive ward called the Cockpit.

A gatehouse originally stood at the north end of the Great Court, but this was incorporated into a new keep, begun *c*.1170 by Conan, 5th Lord of Richmond, and completed by King Henry II, who took possession of the castle after Conan's death in 1171. In the 14th century, John, Duke of Brittany, carried out some improvements, adding

---

THE CONQUEROR'S NORTHERN EXCURSIONS

King William travelled north in 1068 to deal with a threatened revolt. In the Anglo-Scandinavian city of York, he founded two motte-and-bailey castles, now known as Clifford's Tower and Baille Hill. On his way, he established castles at Warwick and Nottingham, and on the way back south built castles at Lincoln, Huntingdon and Cambridge. He returned to York in early 1069 to relieve the castles and again later the same year to unleash the celebrated 'Harrying of the North' in the face of Danish raids and English insurrection. He refortified both York castles and celebrated Christmas 1069, the third anniversary of his coronation day, in Clifford's Tower.

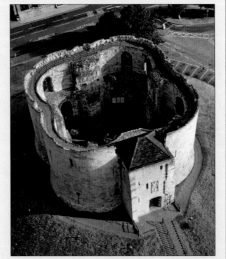

Above: Clifford's Tower, York. It takes its name from Roger de Clifford, hanged there in 1322 for disloyalty to Edward II.

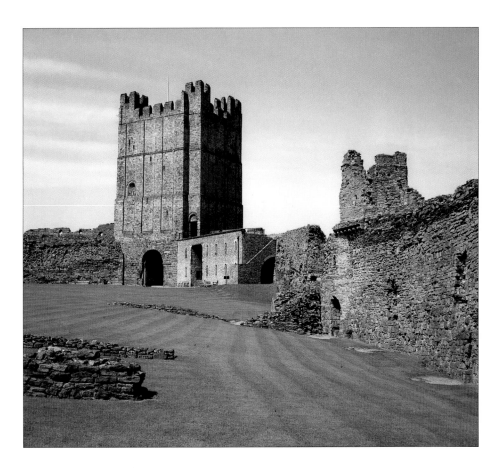

Above: Richmond's 12th-century keep has walls 11ft (3.4m) thick. The arch at its foot may be part of the original gatehouse.

a first-floor Great Chamber and chapel on the northern side of Scolland's Hall and raising the height of the curtain walls and some of the towers.

The castle is of great interest to archaeological historians because it was built with a keep-hall and a curtain wall but without any motte at a time when the Normans were building motte-and-bailey castles. At Richmond, the design was adapted to the location, which, due to its hilltop and riverside location, enjoyed excellent natural defences. Scolland's Hall is the second oldest surviving stone keep in England, after that at Chepstow Castle.

ROYAL RICHMOND

The earldom of Richmond has a famous history and many royal associations. Edward IV's brother, Richard of Gloucester, was Earl of Richmond and held on to the title after he became King Richard III. Henry VII took the title and then bestowed it upon his favourite palace of Sheen by the River Thames in Surrey, the palace he rebuilt following a calamitous fire of Christmas 1498. But the original Richmond Castle had a largely uneventful history. It was not attacked or besieged during either the Wars of the Roses or the English Civil War. Indeed, it was in a ruinous state as early as the mid–16th century.

NORMAN POWER

Other major Norman castles in northern England included the one at Bamburgh, ancient capital of the kings of Northumberland. Little today remains of the Norman fortifications, which may have been built by William the Conqueror in the 1070s; the castle underwent major restoration and rebuilding in the 18th and 19th centuries. The Conqueror also founded another once-significant castle at Lincoln. Begun in 1068, it was built in the south-west part of the walled city established by the Romans. The castle had stone walls from at least 1115, with gateways to east and west and two keep towers on the southern edge.

At Durham, the Normans built a magnificent motte-and-bailey castle to protect the Bishop of Durham, of which only the crypt chapel and part of the gatehouse survive. By the 1140s, Durham Castle consisted of a timber tower on the motte, with a stone curtain wall around the mound; in the bailey stood a chapel, a hall and a chamber block. The proud Norman Romanesque Cathedral, begun in 1093, already stood alongside the castle.

Below: Richmond Castle's isolated position meant that it did not play a significant part in any national conflicts.

CHAPTER TWO

PLANTAGENET MIGHT

1154–1307

The formidable warrior-king Edward I (1239–1307) was the greatest royal castle-builder in English history. He was memorialized on his tombstone as *Scotorum Malleus* ('the Hammer of the Scots') for his battle exploits beyond England's northern border, but he is also remembered for the brutally efficient campaigns he fought in Wales and the network of great castles he erected to impose English rule there. Of the ten castles Edward built during his campaigns against the Welsh, those of Beaumaris, Caernarvon and Harlech are lauded as elegant and innovative examples of the art of castle-building.

Before his accession to the throne, Edward travelled to the Holy Land on Crusade in 1271–2. There, he saw and admired Crusader castles, learning much from their 'concentric' design. The castles had two concentric sets of walls: troops on the higher inner walls could defend the outer walls that they overlooked, but, if necessary, could withdraw within the inner stronghold. On his way back from the East, Edward stopped in Savoy (France), where he met an ambitious castle-builder who had established his reputation by building the widely admired stronghold of St Georges d'Espéranche for Edward I's uncle, Count Philip I of Savoy. Called Master James of St Georges in honour of Count Philip's castle, he became Edward's chief military architect. As Master of the King's Works in Wales, he was largely responsible for the magnificent ring of 'Edwardian' castles erected there.

Left: Symbol of an English king's power in Wales. The eight drum towers and high curtain wall of Conway Castle dominate the shore of the estuary.

ORFORD CASTLE
AND CYLINDRICAL KEEPS

Orford in Suffolk was once on the coast, but now the Orford Ness shingle bank intervenes between the village and the sea. The castle was built by King Henry II, both as a coastal defence against possible invasion and to strengthen the king's hand against the troublesome Earl of Norfolk, Hugh Bigod. Happily for the king, Orford Castle was finished in 1173, just in time to provide a royal stronghold in the face of a rebellion in Suffolk, supported by Bigod, in 1173–4. Following Henry's victory over the rebels, he destroyed Bigod's castles at Framlingham, Bungay, Thetford and Walton.

EXPERIMENTAL KEEPS

The keep, or tower, at Orford was polygonal (many-sided). Three rectangular turrets adjoined the keep, one of which had a forebuilding attached.

Below: The thick wall, round mural towers and outer gatehouse complement the vast circular keep at Pembroke Castle.

In the later 12th and early 13th centuries, castle-builders experimented with new forms for the keep, the main stronghold of the castle. As the techniques and weapons of siege warfare developed during the 12th century, the traditional rectangular keep proved unsatisfactory in two ways: it was vulnerable to attack (its corners could be undermined or destroyed, as at Rochester, making it unstable), while its rectangular shape restricted the defenders' field of fire.

At Orford, the keep's inner design was also experimental. Above the basement, with its own well, were two self-contained residential quarters on the first and second floors, each with kitchen, chambers, garderobe and spacious circular hall. The upper 'apartment' was very grand and evidently intended for the king himself. The forebuilding, on the southern side, contained the entrance way on the ground floor, and the chapel on an upper level between the first and second floors of the main tower. Today, only the keep survives at Orford, but originally it

Above: The turrets of the polygonal keep at Orford are 90ft (27m) tall. The keep is all that survives of a once substantial castle.

stood within a large bailey, or enclosure, surrounded by a defensive wall set with rectangular defensive towers.

The design of the keep at Orford is unusual among English castles. As builders moved on from the 'square' (rectangular) keep, they more often built 'cylindrical' (circular) rather than polygonal towers.

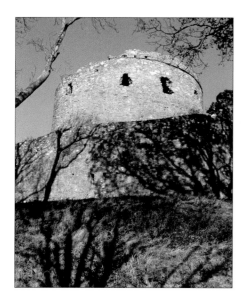

Above: Dundrum Castle is one of John de Courcy's finest castles, set high on a hill overlooking Dundrum Bay.

CONISBROUGH CASTLE

Henry II's illegitimate half-brother, Hamelin Plantagenet, built a splendid keep at Conisbrough, in Yorkshire, in the 1180s. The castle at Conisbrough had been established a little over a century earlier by William de Warenne, a close friend of William the Conqueror. It came into Hamelin's hands on his marriage to Isabel, Warenne's descendant and heiress, in 1164. Hamelin built a circular tower-keep surrounded by six turrets that rise above the main tower to provide elevated defensive positions. These buttress towers are therefore similar to the ones built around ten years earlier at Orford. Archaeological historians also see a fore-runner to the Conisbrough keep in Earl Hamelin's fortified cylindrical keep at Mortemer in Normandy.

At Conisbrough, the keep stood in the north-eastern part of an extensive bailey, surrounded by a thick curtain wall set with semicircular turrets. Within the tower was a basement with a well, a first-floor storage area and residential quarters on the second and third floors – a hall (second floor) beneath a chamber

Right: At Conisbrough Castle in Yorkshire, the cylindrical keep, with its six wedge-shaped buttresses, is 100ft (30m) in height.

(third floor), both luxuriously fitted with fireplace, garderobe and washbasin. Adjoining the chamber, in the easterly turret, was a splendid chapel.

PEMBROKE AND DUNDRUM

Other fine cylindrical keeps were built in the late 12th century at Pembroke in South Wales and at Dundrum (then Rath) in Co Down, on the east coast of Northern Ireland. Built in the years either side of 1200 by William Marshall, Earl of Pembroke, the castle at Pembroke was on the site of an 11th-century stronghold raised by Roger, Earl of Montgomery and Norman Lord of Dyfed. The keep is 75ft (23m) high, with a basement beneath three floors of residential apartments and a domed stone roof. It has a large gatehouse and barbican tower – part of an extensive curtain wall that encloses a sizeable bailey. Pembroke was South Wales's strongest castle. It also has a significant place in history as the birthplace of Henry Richmond, the future King Henry VII.

Dundrum Castle was built by John de Courcy, a Somerset knight who travelled to Ireland in 1171 as part of the Norman incursion and, pushing north on his own, conquered parts of Ulster.

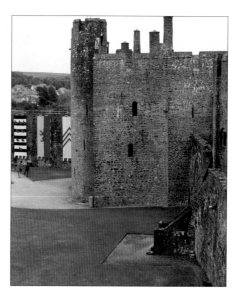

Above: The impressive courtyard at Pembroke Castle is so big that the whole of Harlech Castle could fit within it.

De Courcy established the castle in a formidable position, on the site of a former Celtic fort atop a 200ft (60m) hill overlooking Dundrum Bay. His cylindrical keep was 52ft (16m) high and contained two storeys above a basement. The walls were 8ft (2.5m) thick and in places contained passageways and chambers. The castle's boundary was defined by an imposing curtain wall that ran around the edge of the flattened hilltop.

FRAMLINGHAM CASTLE
THE THIRTEEN TOWERS

The construction of the first castle at Framlingham is traditionally credited to the Norman knight Roger de Bigod, who fought in William the Conqueror's army at Hastings and was rewarded with extensive landholdings. Later, he received the Framlingham estate from Henry I in 1101. Following his death six years later, the castle and land passed first to his eldest son, William, and then, after William died in the '*White Ship* disaster' in 1120, to Roger's second son, Hugh.

Hugh, the powerful and fiercely independent 1st Earl of Norfolk, provoked the wrath of King Henry II, as a result of which the castle of Framlingham was first confiscated by the Crown in 1157–65 and then partially destroyed in 1175, following the failure of a revolt (in which Hugh took part) in 1173–4.

THE CURRENT CASTLE

Hugh's son Roger, 2nd Earl of Norfolk, built Framlingham in its current form in 1190–1210. Earl Roger's design for Framlingham did away with the fortified keep altogether. Instead, probably in tribute to the Byzantine fortresses seen and admired by English knights on

Crusade, the castle's main fortification was a curtain wall containing 13 towers. This enclosed an extensive inner bailey and was complemented by earthwork defences surrounding an even larger outer bailey to the south, west and east. It appears that these were never rebuilt in stone. Additional defence was

Below: The rather inappropriate ornamental chimneys in the courtyard at Framlingham were added in the early 16th century by the castle's then owners, the dukes of Norfolk.

Above: Framlingham is a castle without a keep. Its strength lay in the 13 mural towers in the 44ft (13m) high wall.

provided by an artificial lake, on the castle's western side, created by damming the nearby river. In the inner bailey, Earl Roger built a Great Hall, which in later years was partially demolished and used as a poorhouse.

ROYAL VISITS

King John was entertained at Framlingham Castle in 1213. Three years later, he besieged and captured the Bigod stronghold in the course of the civil war that ended his reign. The castle was returned to the ownership of the Bigods, who later served as Marshals of England, but after once more falling foul of the Crown, they were finally removed from office and relieved of all their landholdings by King Edward I (r.1272–1307).

In 1553, at a time when the castle had been forfeited by the dukes of Norfolk to the Crown, Mary Tudor was staying at Framlingham when she received the news that she had become Queen of England.

CARRICKFERGUS CASTLE
THE NORMANS IN IRELAND

Situated on a rocky outcrop overlooking Belfast Lough is Carrickfergus Castle, which is celebrated as the most complete surviving early medieval castle in the whole of Ireland. John de Courcy, Norman knight and builder of Dundrum Castle in Co Down, built the earliest part of the castle (later its inner ward) in the 1180s.

CASTLE CONSTRUCTION

De Courcy was defeated by Hugh de Lacy, Earl of Ulster, at Carrickfergus. He took possession of the castle, and began work on a massive four-storey rectangular keep some 90ft (27m) high, with a principal chamber measuring 40 x 38ft (12 x 11.5m). De Lacy doubled the size of the castle by enclosing the remainder of the peninsula and raised a substantial curtain wall with projecting towers, arranged to allow for covering arrow fire. Architectural historians compare the layout of the curtain wall and its towers to that at Framlingham. Like Framlingham, Carrickfergus was besieged and captured by King John and passed to the Crown.

Below: The entrance to the four-storey keep at Carrickfergus is on the second floor.

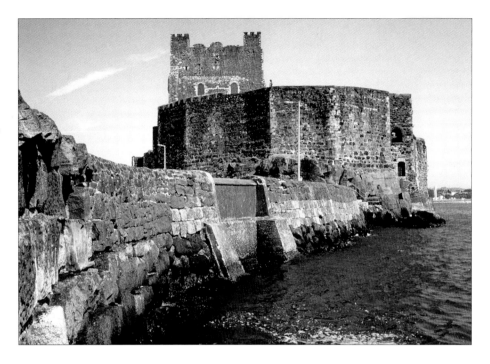

The distinctive gatehouse at Carrickfergus had flanking towers and a high arch that supported a wooden platform used by the defenders. It was added *c*.1250, when the curtain wall enclosing the outer ward was raised.

SCOTTISH BESIEGERS

In 1315, Carrickfergus was besieged by the army of Edward Bruce, brother of King Robert I of Scots. Edward led a Scots force into Ireland that year and was proclaimed High King in 1316; but despite the arrival of reinforcements commanded by his royal brother, he was defeated and killed by Ireland's English rulers in 1318. At Carrickfergus, the English garrison withstood the siege for a full year, apparently forced to eat the flesh of eight dead Scottish prisoners to fend off starvation. However, the castle finally fell to Robert Bruce himself.

Almost 400 years later, the castle played a role in the 'Williamite War', fought to decide the future of the English monarchy after the deposition of King James II and his replacement by Prince William of Orange as William III.

Above: Carrickfergus Castle commanded the waters of Belfast Lough and protected the walled town that grew up alongside it.

In 1690, the 'Williamite' army under General Schomberg besieged and captured the castle. The following year, William himself landed at Carrickfergus to lead the campaign that ended in his victory at the Battle of the Boyne.

Below: The massive walls of Carrickfergus Castle are over 3ft (1m) thick.

MIDDLEHAM CASTLE
HOME OF RICHARD III

In some places the square keep remained in favour. At Middleham in North Yorkshire, *c.*1150–70, Robert FitzRanulph built one of the largest square keeps in western Europe, measuring 110 x 80ft (33.5 x 24m), with walls 12ft (3.5m) thick. Even in its ruinous condition today, it rises to a height of 66ft (20m). Architectural historians use the term 'hall-keep castles' for fortified buildings such as Middleham, which are dominated by substantial keeps containing large halls.

At Middleham, the keep was built close to an earlier castle, an earthwork motte-and-bailey fortification constructed in the last decade or so of the 11th century by Alan Rufus, first Norman Lord of Richmond, or his brother Ribald. The remains of this fortification, now known as 'William's Hill', can be examined today around 500 yards (460m) to the south-west of the main castle.

Below: The remains of Robert FitzRanulph's great square keep (centre back) still dominate the ruined castle at Middleham.

A KING AT HOME IN MIDDLEHAM CASTLE

Richard III loved Middleham Castle. It was the home of his wife, Anne, daughter of Richard Neville ('Warwick the Kingmaker'), and they lived there with her mother, the Countess of Warwick, and Richard and Anne's son, Prince Edward, who was born in the castle's south-west tower (henceforth known as the Prince's Tower) in 1473. It was at Middleham, on 9 April 1484, that Edward died aged just ten, the year before his father was killed at Bosworth Field.

Right: Richard III (1452–85) is often assumed to have been responsible for the murder of the Princes in the Tower.

FAVOURED ROYAL CASTLE

Middleham Castle was a residence fit for a king. Indeed, it later became a favoured royal residence in the 15th century as the home of Richard III and his wife, Anne. Although its builder, Robert FitzRanulph, Ribald's grandson, had close family ties to the lordship of Richmond, he came from only a minor branch of the family, which makes the grandeur of Middleham Castle therefore somewhat surprising.

The keep's two storeys were constructed above a vaulted basement with two wells. The ground floor was occupied by a large kitchen and an extensive cellar-pantry; two circular stone pits are thought to have been used for keeping live fish prior to their preparation for the table. A circular stair in the south-east corner led up to the first floor, which contained a buttery, pantry, small chapel and the Great Hall in its eastern half; beyond a central wall in the western half was a Great Chamber and a privy or private chamber for the Lord of Middleham's personal use. The Great Hall was used both for feasting and as a law court.

DEFENDED STAIRWAY

The keep's main entrance was on the first floor, approached by a heavily fortified stone staircase (now destroyed) on the building's east face. Anyone approaching the keep had to gain access via a manned gateway at the foot of the

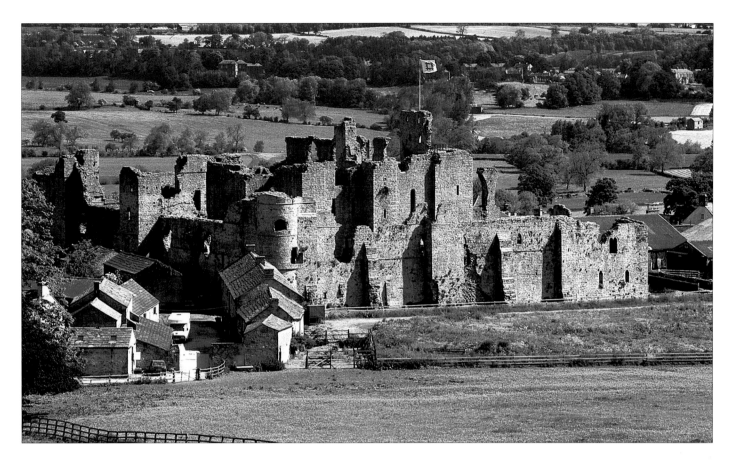

Above: The compact castle at Middleham is square. Although once luxuriously fitted as a palace, it was also a sturdy fortress.

stairs, then pass through another guarded gatehouse halfway up the stairs, and a third at the top of the stairs. All the way up, people climbing the stairs could be watched or, if need be, attacked from a defensive wall with a wall-walk along the top and also from the battlements on top of the keep.

LATER ALTERATIONS

From 1270 onward, the castle was in the hands of a branch of the Neville family, whose descendants later rose to great prominence in the north and, indeed, nationally. Under the Nevilles, a curtain wall was added around the keep in the late 13th century. A three-storey gatehouse with battlements and a projecting 'gallery' from which defenders could throw missiles or pour boiling oil on attacking forces was built in the 15th century. The castle's four towers were built and gradually developed in stages from the 13th to the 15th centuries.

In the 13th century, a substantial three-storey building was raised on the eastern side of the keep, linking it to the castle's eastern wall. It contained two floors of living quarters and a large chapel on the third floor to replace the rather small chapel originally provided within the main keep.

LUXURIOUS ACCOMMODATION

In the late 14th century, Ralph Neville, created Earl of Westmoreland by Richard II, constructed a series of residential chambers within the castle's thick curtain wall to supplement the accommodation provided in the keep. Ralph had a total of 23 children, including 14 by his second wife, Joan Beaufort, the illegitimate daughter of John of Gaunt. In his time, King Henry IV stayed at Middleham Castle and was reportedly impressed by the luxurious accommodation provided.

Ralph's descendant Richard Neville, Earl of Warwick, was the celebrated 'Warwick the Kingmaker', a power-broker during the Wars of the Roses. On his death at the Battle of Barnet on

Easter Sunday, 1471, Middleham Castle passed to Edward IV, who gave it to his brother Richard, Duke of Gloucester, subsequently King Richard III.

Below: Middleham's keep's original staircase has collapsed, but modern steps allow visitors to climb up for views of the town and surrounding Yorkshire countryside.

TINTAGEL CASTLE
KING ARTHUR'S BIRTHPLACE

The ruins of Tintagel Castle in north Cornwall, on a headland and adjacent outcrop, are among the most romantic military remains in Britain. Most of what is visible dates from the 13th century, but the castle's name is forever associated with the story of King Arthur of Camelot, the legendary king of Britain usually associated with a historical Celtic prince of the 5th–6th centuries AD.

THE ARTHURIAN LEGEND

It was in Tintagel Castle, according to the 12th-century Welsh chronicler Geoffrey of Monmouth, that Arthur was conceived. The magician Merlin transformed Uther Pendragon, King of Britain, into the likeness of Gorlois, Duke of Cornwall, so that he could lie with Gorlois's ravishing wife, Ygerna. The result was Arthur, who may also have been born at Tintagel. Later, he became – according to the legend – Britain's greatest king, Celtic defeater of the Saxons, embodiment of chivalric

Below: This watercolour of the remains of Tintagel Castle is by 19th-century American artist, William Trost Richards.

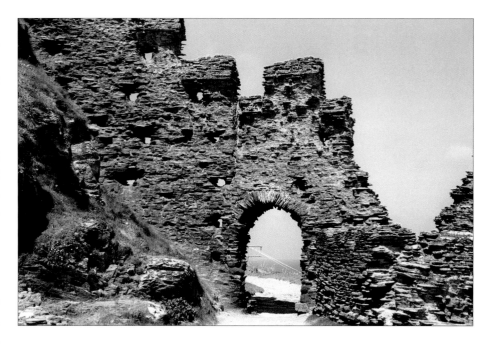

virtue, lord of Camelot and leader of the knights of the Round Table. Some versions of his legend suggest that he himself held court at Tintagel.

FROM MONASTERY TO RUIN

The headland at Tintagel may have been used as an Iron Age Celtic fortress or later as a Saxon fort, but no evidence remains of these fortifications. Tintagel was certainly the site of a monastic community established by the Celtic Christian missionary St Juliot in the

Above: Gateway to a romantic past? Tintagel's dramatic setting encourages visions of Merlin, Arthur and Ygerna.

early 6th century, and there are traces of a monastic cell (dwelling) and of an underfloor heating system thought to have been used by the monks.

In 1145, Reginald, an illegitimate son of Henry I, built a castle on the headland; the chapel and Great Hall are believed to survive from his time. His castle was extended by Richard, 1st Earl of Cornwall and Knight of the Holy Roman Empire. Most of the surviving castle buildings are from his stronghold.

The gate and upper ward of the castle were constructed on the headland, while a separate ward containing the Great Hall stood on the outcrop, which could be reached by a very narrow rock causeway. This has since been eroded by the sea, and access to the outcrop is now by steps cut into the rock.

Tintagel Castle fell into ruins after Earl Richard's time, and it was for many years a largely unregarded, if beautifully situated, ruin. However, the 19th-century revival of interest in Arthurian legend put the castle back on the map.

WINCHESTER GREAT HALL
AND THE ROUND TABLE

Winchester, in Hampshire, southern England, was the capital of the Anglo-Saxon kingdom of Wessex and the burial place of kings, including Alfred and Canute II. It remained England's principal city until the 12th century.

A Norman castle was built there soon after the Conquest, in the reign of King William I the Conqueror. King Henry III was born in the castle, on 1 October 1207, and in his time the Norman castle was rebuilt after having fallen into disrepair during King John's reign. Henry was a man of culture and refinement, whose reign saw the major rebuilding of Westminster Palace and Abbey, Windsor Castle and the construction of magnificent English cathedrals at Lincoln, Wells, Salisbury and St Alban's. At Winchester, the Great Hall is all that survives of his work.

ARTHUR'S ROUND TABLE

A magnificent round table that hangs on the wall of the Winchester Great Hall was for many years identified as the Round Table of King Arthur of Camelot. The table, 18ft (5.5m) in diameter and 2,640lb (1,200kg) in weight, is decorated with the names of the 24 knights of Arthur's company and a portrait of the king himself. According to the *Roman de Brut* (1155), one of the early medieval romances that developed the Arthurian legend, Arthur introduced a round table so that none of the knights could claim precedence over any other. Historians have established that the table in question was not made until the 14th century and was decorated in the reign of Henry VIII, who had a keen interest in knightly exploits, the Arthurian story and the chivalric tradition.

THE KING'S HALL

The Winchester Great Hall was an early example of a new development in such buildings, a movement away from the dark and shadowy halls of the 12th century to a lighter, more elegant design. Henry's hall contained columns of Purbeck stone, fashionable plate tracery windows and pointed arches. Its walls were plastered and decorated in brilliant colours. When he was in Winchester, Henry used the hall for dining, sitting in council with leading barons and

Above: The legend of King Arthur's round table inspired this vast 14th-century tribute, now hung in the Great Hall at Winchester.

clergy and as a courtroom. It is a fine example of the early English Gothic style of architecture.

In the reign of Henry's successor, Edward I, a major fire destroyed most of the royal apartments at Winchester in 1302. Edward and Queen Margaret, his second wife, were in residence at the time and were almost burned alive.

CAERPHILLY CASTLE
CONCENTRIC DEFENCES

The forbidding Caerphilly Castle in Glamorgan, South Wales, was built in 1271–c.1280 by Gilbert de Clare (1243–95), Lord of Glamorgan and one of the most powerful men in the realm. It covers 30 acres (12ha), and is the largest castle in Wales, as well as the second largest British castle, after Windsor. Both in size and in the splendour of its residential quarters, Caerphilly Castle rivalled the great Welsh strongholds, such as Beaumaris and Harlech, built shortly after by King Edward. It is rightly regarded by historians and architects as one of the most splendid castles in all Europe and as one of the finest medieval buildings erected in the British Isles.

As a 'Marcher Lord' (a descendant of the Norman lords created by William the Conqueror to subdue the natives in the Welsh Marches), de Clare had the right to build castles without royal licence and to wage war on his own behalf. He had become a man of great wealth when he inherited the earldom of Gloucester in 1262 and had driven Welsh prince Gruffudd ap Rhys out of upland Glamorgan in 1266.

LLYWELYN'S THREAT

De Clare's vast castle at Caerphilly, begun at the very end of Henry III's reign when the future Edward I was abroad on Crusade, must by its overwhelming size have provoked some misgivings at the royal court. However, de Clare's principal concern was to counter the threat of Welsh prince Llywelyn ap Gruffudd, who had control of much of northern and middle Wales and was aiming to move southwards and capture

Above: Gilbert Clare, Lord of Glamorgan. This Victorian image is based on a near-contemporary stained glass window (c.1340) at Tewkesbury Abbey Church.

Glamorgan. With his powerful siege engines, Llywelyn had in 1270 overrun and destroyed an earlier castle that de Clare had begun to build at Caerphilly.

WALLS OF DEFENCE

The surviving stronghold at Caerphilly is notable as Britain's first truly concentric castle, one with twin defensive walls. The low outer wall has two gatehouses, each with two towers, as well as a water gate in the south front. The inner wall is rectangular, fortified with one gatehouse facing east and one facing west, a great kitchen tower and a tower at each of the corners of the rectangle.

THE CONCENTRIC CASTLE

A stronghold with two defensive boundaries (an outer wall overlooked and protected by a taller and stronger inner round of fortifications) is known as a concentric castle. The design was used by the Romans and put to very effective use in Crusader castles, such as Krak des Chevaliers in Syria. Shortly after the construction of Caerphilly, Edward I and his chief architect, Master James of St Georges, used the concentric design in the castle of Beaumaris, Anglesey, in 1295.

Below: This aerial view of Caerphilly shows impressive double walls – with higher inner fortifications – and extensive water defences.

Above: As part of a programme of modern repairs to Caerphilly Castle begun c.1870 by John Crichton Stuart, the 3rd Marquess of Bute, the water defences were restored by reflooding the lake.

Along the south side of the inner rectangle were the Great Hall and luxuriously appointed state apartments. The Great Hall was remodelled in 1322–6, when the castle was in the possession of Hugh le Despenser the Younger, favourite of Edward II.

The castle's main stronghold was the eastern gatehouse of the inner wall, intended as the residence of the castle constable. Its entrance passage could be closed with door and portcullis towards both the outer ward (the area within the outer wall, but outside the inner wall) and the inner ward (the area enclosed by the inner wall), and so could be defended from both directions. If the castle were overrun, its remaining defenders could retreat to this gatehouse.

The castle's forbidding stone defences were supplemented by a vast encircling moat that was probably inspired by the siege of Kenilworth Castle in 1266, in which its water defences greatly prolonged the encounter, which de Clare witnessed.

CAERPHILLY'S LEANING TOWER

Caerphilly's south-eastern tower leans dramatically 9ft (2.75m) from the perpendicular. The most likely explanation for this is that it was partially demolished during the English Civil War by parliamentarian forces determined to spoil the castle defences.

A more romantic tale maintains that when Edward II, at the close of his reign, took refuge in Caerphilly Castle, then held by his favourite Hugh le Despenser, his estranged wife, Queen Isabella, pursued him with armed force. Edward moved on, but Isabella besieged the castle and captured the tower, later setting off a vast explosion that almost brought it down.

RESTORATION

In the early part of the 15th century, Owain Glyndwr held Caerphilly Castle in the course of his failed revolt against Henry IV. By 1536, the castle had become derelict, except for one part, which remained in use as a prison. The stronghold was restored c.1870 by the 3rd Marquess of Bute, the builder-restorer of Cardiff Castle and Castell Coch, and then by his son, the 4th Marquess, in the early 20th century. The 5th Marquess placed Caerphilly Castle in state care in 1950.

Below: Beyond the Lower Eastern Gatehouse at Caerphilly is the Inner East Gate, with the celebrated leaning tower to the left.

CAERNARVON CASTLE
CONSTANTINOPLE'S INFLUENCE

In 1283, Edward I began building an impressive castle and walled town at Caernarvon in North Wales, as a symbol of his conquest of the Welsh. The king was fresh from triumph in the Second Welsh War (1282–3), in which he had slain Welsh prince Llywelyn ap Gruffudd and captured his brother Dafydd, Prince of Gwynedd.

STRATEGIC POSITION

As he prepared to establish English government in Wales, Edward wanted to make a triumphalist expression of his imperial ambitions at Caernarvon. He chose the town because it was an ancient stronghold for the princes of Gwynedd and because of its strategic position overlooking the Menai Straits, where the River Seoint reaches the sea, and controlling access to Snowdonia – but principally because it was the site of Roman Segontium, which had defended the north-west frontier of the empire.

Below: With his magnificent fortress at Caernarvon, Edward wanted to impress his regal power on his new Welsh subjects.

AN EMPEROR'S DREAM CASTLE

In appearance and design, Caernarvon is quite different to the other great castles Edward raised in Wales, at Harlech, Conway and Beaumaris. Caernarvon has polygonal rather than circular drum towers, and cross-banded masonry (alternate strips of light and dark stone) in the defensive walls.

Edward built Caernarvon as the fulfilment of a dream traditionally said to have come to Roman Emperor Magnus Maximus, son of Constantine I, in which he travelled to a land of mountains and found there a marvellous fortress with walls of varied hues, containing an ivory throne capped with golden eagles. The polygonal towers and cross-banded walls were apparently a homage to the Theodosian Wall at Constantinople, which Edward and his chief architect, Master James of St Georges, had seen while on Crusade.

King Edward and Master James incorporated into the castle an 11th-century Norman motte-and-bailey fortification built at Caernarvon by Hugh, Earl of Chester. In this way, Edward made the symbolic statement

Above: The towers of Caernarvon have stood proud for centuries. This watercolour shows the Eagle Tower c.1850.

HISTORY TIMELINE

1294 The castle is besieged by land forces in the Welsh uprising led by Madog ap Llewelyn; the benefit of its maritime location is proven as the garrison takes in supplies by sea and survives until a relieving army arrives in the spring of 1295.

1323 The castle assumes roughly its modern form, after 40 years' building.

1399 Richard II visits. Furnishings and decorations must be unfinished, for he has to sleep on straw.

1401-3 Owen Glendower tries unsuccessfully three times to take the castle. The third time, he uses heavy siege machinery, but is still repulsed by a garrison of only 28 men.

1646 During the English Civil War, the castle, garrisoned by Royalists, is captured by Major-General Mytton for the Parliamentarians.

*c.***1890** After centuries of neglect, the castle is repaired.

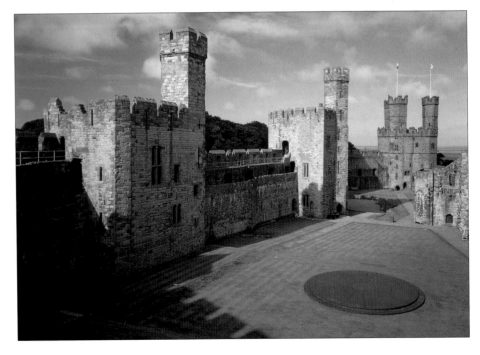

that his claim to Wales was merely the renewal of an ancient right established by the Normans. A walled borough, or town, was built alongside the castle, the two making a heavily fortified seat for English royal government in Wales. Defences were strengthened further by the tidal waters that the castle overlooks: originally the castle and town stood on a peninsula that was almost completely surrounded by water. The castle has an irregular oblong design because it was built in the shape of the rock it occupies.

At the western end of the castle stands the majestic Eagle Tower, at 124ft (38m) high one of the tallest single towers erected in the Middle Ages. When first built, it had a stone eagle on each of its three turrets. The tower contained the splendid residence of the castle's keeper, the Justiciar (or regent) of North Wales.

BUILT FOR DEFENCE

At Caernarvon, Master James designed a forbidding fortress. Defenders in the 13 polygonal towers could cover the entire circumference of the castle. In the south front, soldiers and archers could rain weapons on attackers from two 'firing galleries' that ran, one above the other, right along the wall. There were two main gateways: at the east end, the Queen's Gate gave into the inner bailey

ENGLISH PRINCE OF WALES

On 25 April 1284, Edward I's wife, Queen Eleanor, gave birth to their first-born son at Caernarvon. According to tradition, he then presented the infant to his Welsh subjects as their next ruler, pointing out that the baby was currently without blame, had been born in Wales and spoke not a single word of English. Seven years later, again at Caernarvon, the boy was invested as Prince of Wales. In 1911, in a romanticized 'medieval' ceremony, Edward, eldest son of George V, was invested as Prince of Wales in the castle. The ceremony was devised for Prince Edward and his father by David

Right: Famous for his castle-building and battlefield exploits, Edward I also recodified English common law.

Lloyd George, MP for Caernarvon. Some 58 years later, Queen Elizabeth II's eldest son, Charles, was invested as Prince of Wales at Caernarvon on 1 July 1969.

by way of a drawbridge; on the north front, the King's Gate gave access to the castle from the walled town. The latter had impressive defences, for it contained six portcullises and five doors.

Master James' plan was for the enclosure within the castle walls to be divided across the middle by the gate-house, but the interior of the castle was never completed, as was a tower on the

mound of the Norman castle within the walls. Building work on the castle went on until 1330, yet much of it was left unfinished. In its surviving form, it is the shell of a magnificent fortress.

Below: Coastal stronghold of Caernarvon. Edward built his major Welsh fortresses on the coast because the Welsh intercepted land supplies and he needed access to the sea.

CONWAY CASTLE
DRUM TOWERS

The castle and walled town of Conway in North Wales were built by King Edward I in just five years (1283–8). Again designed by Edward's great architect, Master James of St Georges, the castle comprises eight massive drum towers linked by a high curtain wall that is 15ft (4.5m) thick in parts. The sturdy walls of the adjacent town contain three gates and 21 strong towers; on average 24ft (7.5m) in thickness, they run for over ¾ mile (0.5km). They survive in good condition over seven centuries later.

RING OF STONE

Conway was part of the ring of Welsh castles planned by King Edward I to impose English rule, enforced by English-garrisoned strongholds, on the Welsh. At Conway, however, in contrast to Beaumaris, Caernarvon and Harlech, Master James elected not to raise strongly fortified gatehouses with twin

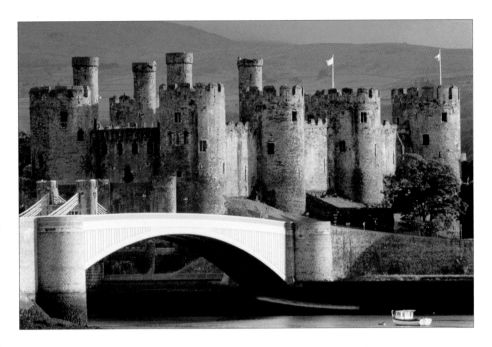

**MASTER JAMES
OF ST GEORGES**

Edward's chief architect, the builder of the 'Edwardian' castles of North Wales, was Master James of St Georges (c.1230–c.1308). A native of Savoy, Master James took his full title from the magnificent castle of St Georges d'Espéranche, which he built for Edward I's friend and relative, Count Philip of Savoy. Like the castle at Caernarvon, St Georges d'Espéranche had polygonal towers. Master James built eight Welsh castles for Edward I: Aberystwyth, Beaumaris, Builth, Caernarvon, Conway, Flint, Harlech and Rhuddlan. Master James won a position of great eminence, was styled Master of the King's Works in Wales, and earned the then vast amount of three shillings a day.

---

towers. The drum towers in the castle walls defended both western and eastern entrances to the castle and made extra fortifications on the gate unnecessary.

INNER AND OUTER WARDS

Like Caernarvon, the castle at Conway has a narrow, elongated shape because it was designed to fit the rock on which it stands: a high promontory in a commanding position alongside the tidal waters of the river estuary. Within the high defensive walls, the castle was divided by a gateway into the outer and inner wards on an east–west axis. Access from the town was via a drawbridge across the moat at the north-western end of the rock. A steep flight of steps led into the west barbican (outer defence), which was defended by the western-most two of the castle's eight great towers. From there a gateway led into the outer ward, which contained the kitchen, stables and Great Hall. The constable had his quarters in the great towers overlooking the west barbican.

Right: Conway Castle's intimidating towers and vast curtain wall appear to grow naturally from the rocky outcrop on which they stand.

Above: Stephenson's rail and Telford's road bridge run past Edward I's castle at Conway.

The smaller inner ward was the heart of the castle, containing the royal quarters: the King's Hall, Privy Chamber and Presence Chamber. The castle's south-east tower housed the king's sleeping rooms, while the north-east tower contained a well-appointed chapel. Beyond was the east barbican and stairs leading down to a water gate.

'BASTIDE' FORTIFIED TOWN

Conway Castle and town were, like Caernarvon and Flint, planned as a single defensive and trading unit.

Edward I had seen the success of building planned towns beside garrisoned castles in English-held Gascony (south-west France), and applied the idea in North Wales. The Welsh towns were planned as centres for the English administration of an occupied country. They were settled with English people, and the Welsh locals were often forbidden to enter the town or to trade with its people, and could risk hanging if found within the walls after sunset.

In 1401, according to tradition, a local carpenter won control of Conway Castle from Henry IV's garrison. Gaining access to the stronghold on Good Friday, when the majority of the defending garrison were at church, he then opened the gates to Welsh rebels, who declared for Owen Glendower, self-styled native Prince of Wales. The occupation itself did not

Below: Looking down to the west from the King's Tower on Conway's outer ward, the remains of the Great Hall lie on the left.

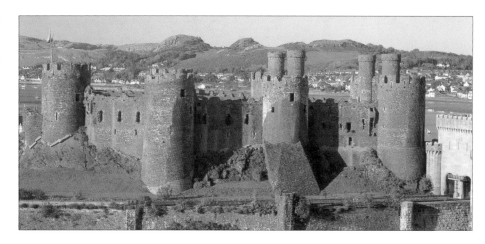

last long, however; Glendower's revolt against Henry IV failed, although subsequently, it is said, most of the rebels were granted pardons.

DECLINE AND RUIN

Over the next two centuries, the castle fell into disrepair. According to a state paper of 1609, it was already 'utterlie decayed', and in this condition was sold for £100 to Viscount Conway. The castle was repaired for use in the Civil War by John Williams, a Conway man

Above: Four of Conway's eight towers guard the castle's outer ward, while the other four protect the inner ward.

who had risen to be Archbishop of York. In the war, Conway was besieged and captured by Parliamentarians commanded by Major-General Mytton and afterwards was slighted. In 1665, the 3rd Earl of Conway reduced the castle to little more than a ruin by removing all the ironwork, lead and timbers. It was restored in the 19th and 20th centuries.

RHUDDLAN, FLINT AND GOODRICH
CASTLES BY THE WATER

Rhuddlan Castle in Denbighshire, North Wales, was begun by King Edward I at the same time as its near-neighbour at Flint, in 1277. Rhuddlan and Flint, the first of the ten castles built by Edward I in Wales, were both raised alongside new towns set within earth-work fortifications. At Rhuddlan, the River Clwyd was diverted and canalized for 2–3 miles (3–5km) to allow seago-ing vessels to approach the newly constructed landing stages, which were built separately for castle and town.

Rhuddlan was a long-established military and royal base. It was originally the setting for a fort built in AD971 by Edward the Elder, son of Alfred the Great, and was afterwards the kingly seat

Below: Loading bay. At Rhuddlan, the smooth waters of a canalized stretch of the Clwyd approach the castle's landing stage.

of Welsh ruler, Gruffydd ap Llywelyn. Gruffydd's stronghold was destroyed by Harold Godwinson in 1063. After the Norman Conquest, a motte-and-bailey castle was built there in 1073 by lead-ing nobleman, Robert of Rhuddlan. In 1276–7, Edward I marched into the region to stamp out the threat posed by Welsh ruler, Llywelyn ap Gruffydd, self-styled 'Prince of Wales'. In the course of this campaign, Edward began the castles at Flint and Rhuddlan, and received the submission of Llywelyn at Rhuddlan in November 1277.

Edward's castle at Rhuddlan, raised around 650–1,000ft (200–300m) north-west of the Norman fortifications, was begun by Master Bertram de Saltu, a Gascon engineer, but finished by Master James of St Georges, to whom the castle is usually attributed. Rhuddlan Castle was built swiftly, and was largely complete by 1280.

Above: The remains of the south tower overlook the inner ward at Rhuddlan.

INNER WARD AND MOAT
The design was for a concentric castle, with a relatively low outer wall that was overlooked by the much more formi-dable fortifications of the inner ward. Beyond the outer wall was an artificial moat, itself protected by a further outer wall on three sides of the castle.

GOODRICH CASTLE: BUILT IN RED SANDSTONE

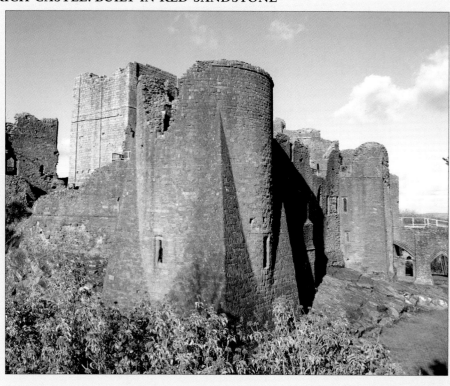

Goodrich Castle in Hereford and Worcester was largely rebuilt by Edward I's uncle, William de Valence, and William's son, Aymer, in the years after 1280. The Valences' castle, which overlooks the River Wye and defends an ancient river ford, incorporates an earlier tower-keep (of the mid-1100s). The Valences rebuilt the curtain wall and added impressive angle towers together with ditches on the east and south sides, and an outer defensive wall to the west and north, with a barbican to the north-east. The barbican, in a half-moon shape, seems to be derived from the similar Lions' Tower raised by Edward I at the Tower of London.

Right: The south-east tower largely hides the square keep (centre left). A modern rail lines the approach to the gatehouse (right).

To the south, however, giving on to the river, a short section was filled with water and used as a dock. In fact, the other three sections of the moat appear to have been kept dry to serve as a defensive ditch.

The symmetrical inner ward took the shape of a diamond. Matching towers rose at the north and south corners of the diamond, and double-towered gate-houses stood at the east and west corners. Within, a Great Hall, chapel, private rooms and kitchens once stood against the curtain wall. The inner fortifications were forbidding, with four-storey towers and walls 9ft (3m) thick, with a plentiful supply of arrow slits for the defenders.

BEYOND THE CASTLE

Four gates led out from the castle's outer ward: the main one leading northwards to the newly built town, another gate giving on to the river, a third gate on to the dock, defended by a rectangular defensive tower, and a fourth, the Friary Gate (later blocked), opening to the south-east.

THE DONJON TOWER AT FLINT

The main strength of Flint Castle, completed with its adjacent town in nine years (1277–86), is its circular great tower at the south-east corner of the rectangular inner ward, which is set apart, surrounded by a moat. Castle historians liken the tower to the celebrated Tour Constance at the French port of Aigues-Mortes, from which Edward set sail with his troops for North Africa, while on Crusade in 1270.

The tower is the donjon, the lord's residence within the castle and the heavily fortified position to which the defenders would fall back as a last resort. It is supplemented by three more towers, one at each angle of the rectangular inner wall. (The French word *donjon* later became the English 'dungeon'; but in its earliest use in England, it signified the lord's dwelling rather than a gloomy jail-room.)

Another notable feature at Flint was the internal arrangement of rooms within the great tower. Above a large circular storage basement, the residential rooms and chapel on the first storey are arranged around a large, central, octagonal shaft, designed to bring light and air to residents. (Originally the building contained a basement and two storeys, although only the first storey now remains.) This arrangement is supposedly unique.

Below: The ruined north-east tower at Flint. The great tower at the south-east corner was complemented by three smaller towers at the other angles of the rectangular inner ward.

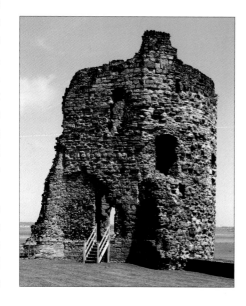

HARLECH CASTLE
IMPREGNABLE FORTRESS

At Harlech, Edward I and Master James of St Georges raised a concentric castle with a great twin-towered gatehouse on top of an imposing, steep-sided 200ft (60m) rock. When Edward and Master James built the castle in the late 13th century, the rock directly over-looked the sea and the tidal estuary of the River Dwyryd. Indeed, there was a landing stage for receiving seaborne supplies, accessed from the castle by a heavily fortified stairway, the 'Way from the Sea'. Today, however, the tidal creek is dry and the sea has retreated more than ½ mile (0.8km). Yet, because an approach up the cliff-like sides of the castle rock would be almost impossible, Harlech Castle retains an almost impregnable aspect – with land attack feasible only from the east. The castle was, in fact, taken four times: in 1404, 1408, 1468 and 1647.

The castle, begun in the summer of 1283 during King Edward I's second military campaign in North Wales, was built at a cost of £9,500 over the seven years to December 1290. At one point, in 1286, Master James had an army of 950 labourers at his disposal.

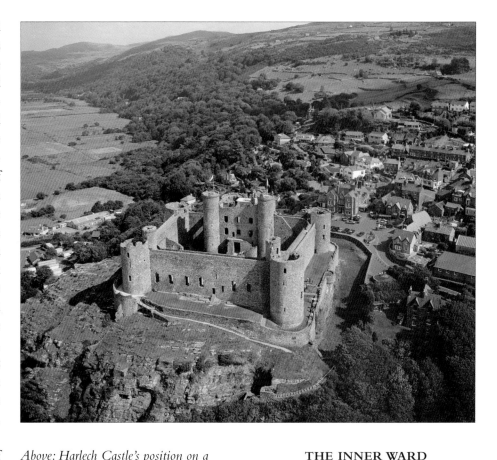

Above: Harlech Castle's position on a hilltop meant that space was tight. The outer ward is narrow and the inner ward small.

Below: Safe within the castle walls, the inner face of the gatehouse at Harlech can risk windows and a gentle staircase.

THE INNER WARD

The castle's outer defences are largely ruined, and the outer ward is very narrow, due to lack of space. However, the inner ward boasts four drum towers and the massively fortified gatehouse facing east. The gatehouse consists of two projecting semi-cylindrical towers flanking a narrow entranceway defended by three portcullises and gates, and seven 'murder holes' from which defenders could launch missiles or scalding water at the attackers.

The gatehouse contained guard-houses on the ground level at either side of the entrance, and on the first floor were the well-appointed quarters of the castle constable. On the second floor were even more luxurious rooms for the use of important visitors, doubtless including King Edward I. Both sets of rooms included a hall, a chamber, a bed-chamber and a private chapel. Although the outer face of the gatehouse presents a stern aspect, its inner walls contain large windows, and there is a fine external

KIDWELLY CASTLE

Where Harlech Castle failed to repulse Owain Glyndwr, Kidwelly Castle in Dyfed succeeded, twice withstanding siege attacks by the 'Prince of Wales' in 1403–05. Kidwelly Castle was originally Norman, built by Roger, Bishop of

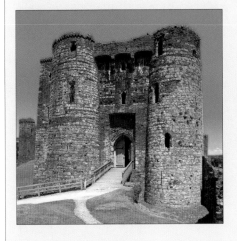

Salisbury and Justiciar of England under Henry I, overlooking and commanding the upper tidal reaches of the River Gwendraeth. After being captured more than once by the Welsh and partially rebuilt by Lord Rhys in 1190, it passed to Edward I's nephew, Henry, Earl of Lancaster, in 1298. Around the inner castle with four drum towers, Henry built a heavily fortified outer defensive wall in imitation of the concentric castles of his uncle and Master James of St Georges. The impressive outer wall had four towers (one of which contained a chapel) and two gatehouses.

Left: The Great Gatehouse at Kidwelly Castle. On the first floor, directly above the gate, was a large and well-appointed hall.

staircase giving access to the constable's apartments, in which Master James, who was made the castle constable in July 1290, lived for the next three years.

There were further, less grand, residential rooms in the towers at the angles of the rectangular inner ward. Functional rooms, such as the Great Hall, buttery, granary, bake house and kitchens, were situated within the walls of the inner ward quadrangle.

HARLECH SIEGES

The castle may have been almost impregnable in the face of violent attack, but it could be vulnerable to being cut off from reinforcements and supplies. If the garrison maintained access to the sea, then all was well: when besieged by the troops of Madog ap Llywelyn in the 1294–5 uprising, the castle defenders received supplies by sea from Ireland. However, when the Welsh rebel and self-styled 'Prince of Wales', Owain Glyndwr, took the castle in 1401, he was able to block all supplies, since a fleet of his French allies was active in the waters beneath the rock while his own troops blocked land access.

During the Wars of the Roses in the 15th century, the castle was garrisoned by men loyal to the Lancastrian cause under Dafydd ap Iuean, and was besieged by a Yorkist army commanded by Lord Herbert, Earl of Pembroke. The garrison withstood immense hardship before surrendering in 1468 – a feat that inspired the marching song *Men of Harlech*. A royalist garrison defended Harlech Castle during the Civil War in the 17th century. Surrendered as late as March 1647, it was the last castle to fall to the Parliamentarian army.

Below: Harlech's rocky heights. The land falls steeply away on all sides save the east, and the position commands superb views.

BEAUMARIS CASTLE
MASTER JAMES' MASTERPIECE

Beaumaris Castle on Anglesey was the last of the great castles built in Wales for Edward I by his chief builder, Master James of St Georges. Although it remained unfinished, it is celebrated today as a triumphant culmination of Edward's two decades of Welsh castle-building. Its plan, an octagon enclosing a rectangle, is lauded as the perfection of the concentric castle design. Set amid meadows rich in bulrushes, with distant views across into Snowdonia, it is also known for the great beauty of its location.

WELSH UPRISING

Beaumaris was begun in the spring of 1295. The previous year, during an uprising led by Llywelyn ap Gruffud's kinsman, Madog ap Llywelyn, Welsh rebels had overrun Anglesey and killed the royal sheriff, Roger de Pulesdon. Edward launched fierce reprisals over the winter of 1294–5 and was still in the area when the building of Beaumaris Castle began.

Below: The northern gate, or Llanfaes Gate, Beaumaris, viewed from the inner ward. A further storey was planned but never built.

THREE LAYERS OF DEFENCE

Built on flat marshy land, the castle had no natural defences, save the sea to the south, and needed to be heavily fortified. The design called for three concentric layers of defence: a moat, 18ft (5.5m) wide and filled with tidal water, and two sets of defensive walls. The octagonal outer wall contained 12 towers and two gatehouses. The rectangular inner wall, in places 15ft (4.5m) thick, contained four round towers (one at each corner), two gatehouses and two D-shaped towers.

Above: Beaumaris dwarfed by Snowdonia. In this view from the north, the waters of the Menai Strait are visible beyond the castle.

The main entrance in the outer wall to the south gave on to the sea at high tide. Known as the Gate-next-the-Sea, it overlooked a small dock area where ships could land supplies at high tide. The second gateway, called the Llanfaes Gate from the name of the Welsh town nearby, opened landwards to the north. The outer wall was lower and less thick than the forbidding inner fortification. The gates in the outer wall were set at an angle to those in the inner one, so that any attacker who succeeded in breaching the outer defences would have to make an awkward turn to the right under fire from the defenders of the inner stronghold. The outer ward, the area between the outer and inner walls, was just a narrow strip of land.

The two imposing inner gatehouses stood in the north and south stretches of the rectangular inner wall. The west and east walls, without gatehouses, contained formidable D-shaped towers, planned as three-storey buildings but never completed beyond the second floor. In addition, a circular tower rose

Above: Stones piled high – the bulk of the castle at Beaumaris and its superb design made up for its lack of natural defences.

A WHITE ELEPHANT

Above: Never finished, but formidable nonetheless - Beaumaris Castle in the 14th century has a moat and double walls.

in each corner of the rectangle. The plans called for lavishly appointed chambers and halls, mainly in the first and second floors of the gatehouses. These were never fully built, but the castle's main room, the Great Hall on the first floor of the north gatehouse, gives an idea of the splendour awaiting the Prince of Wales or the king. The Chapel Tower, also part of the inner walls, contains a magnificently appointed chapel with vaulted ceiling and point windows. Within these formidable walls, the inner ward is surprisingly large, covering ¾ acre (0.3ha).

Edward I poured lavish resources into the work: Master James employed no fewer than 200 quarrymen, 30 smiths and carpenters, 400 masons and 2,000 general labourers. He had spent £6,000 by the autumn of 1295. The bulk of the building was carried out in the three years after 1295; by 1298, royal funds for building were running low, and the king was increasingly focused on events and building works in Scotland and Gascony.

Further building was carried out at Beaumaris beginning in 1306 and continuing intermittently after Edward's death in 1307 until 1330, without ever reaching completion. The castle remains

an example of 'what might have been': a magnificent plan that was never brought to fulfilment.

Moreover, its formidable defences were never needed. Beaumaris, for all its might, saw little military action – for even by the time the castle was begun, Welsh resistance had been almost entirely crushed. Some 200 years later, it was garrisoned by Royalists in the Civil War, but was taken without a struggle by the Parliamentarian scourge of Edward's Welsh castles, Major-General Mytton, on 14 June 1646.

CAERLAVEROCK CASTLE, DUMFRIES

The builders of Caerlaverock were clearly influenced by Beaumaris and Master James's other great concentric castles. Caerlaverock combines a twin-towered gatehouse with two drum towers, the whole laid out to a triangular design within a defensive moat and an earthen rampart. The main defence and final refuge is the gatehouse, which – as at Beaumaris – contained the residential quarters of the castle constable.

Right: Within the castle lie the remains of 18th-century courtyard residences.

CHAPTER THREE

THE FORTIFIED HOUSE

1307–1400

In 1290, wealthy wool merchant Lawrence of Ludlow obtained a royal licence to crenellate his manor at Stokesay in Shropshire. He declared that he needed to fortify the house because of the potential threat of the unruly Welsh just 20 miles (32km) away across the border. In fact, Edward I's forceful campaigns of the 1280s in Wales had effectively stamped out resistance there.

Lawrence's home, Stokesay Castle, was not a castle proper but an early example of a type of building that would become popular with wealthy householders in the 14th and 15th centuries: the fortified manor house. Other splendid examples include Penshurst Place, Hever Castle and Ightham Mote, all in Kent; Broughton Castle in Oxfordshire; and Raby Castle in Co Durham. Many of these buildings were fortified towards the end of the 14th century, when England had seemingly lost control of the English Channel and there were fears that France might invade. At this time (under Richard II) and again in the 15th century (under Henry VI), central authority was weak, so landowners needed to project at least an appearance of strength.

Yet, while fortified manor houses had a degree of defensive strength, none of them was a fortress. The houses may have been well enough defended to deter passing marauders, but they generally could not have withstood an attack by an organized army; they certainly could not have repelled a siege in the way that Rochester Castle almost did, and Kidwelly Castle in Dyfed twice succeeded in doing. The men who built the fortified manor houses put comfort before the needs of defence.

Left: The charming manor house of Ightham Mote, in Kent, combines a crenellated gatehouse and defensive moat with windows and a half-timbered upper storey.

STOKESAY CASTLE
AN ENGLISH STONE HOUSE

Stokesay Castle's name comes from that of a family – Say – who had their dairy farm ('stoke') here from around 1115. Wool merchant Lawrence of Ludlow fortified the house in the early 1290s.

Lawrence's father, John, had purchased the manor in 1281. Earlier, in 1240, the Says had built a tower at the north end of the house's west front. Lawrence added a new upper storey with projecting timberwork, which remarkably survives to this day. He also built a new Great Hall, 34ft (10.3m) high and measuring 52 x 31ft (16 x 9.5m), with partly shuttered, partly glazed windows – proof of his substantial wealth, for at this time glass cost so much that wealthy families with more than one house carried their window panes with them as they moved about. Much of the timberwork survives from the 13th century. The rafters are blackened by the smoke that rose from the chimney-less central hearth to find its way out via the louvres in the roof.

Below: Stokesay Castle's spacious hall is flanked by the north tower (left) and the solar with the turreted south tower (right).

A ROOM FOR RETIRING TO
Attached to the hall on the south side, Lawrence erected the 'solar block', containing a chamber to which the family withdrew from the more public space of the Great Hall. The private chamber, known as a 'solar' because the room was designed with large windows to allow in as much sunlight as possible, was on the upper floor, and reached by an external staircase, while the ground-level space beneath was used for storage.

Above: The magnificent beams of the Great Hall's roof were made from whole trees.

DEFENSIVE ADDITIONS
At the Great Hall's south end, Lawrence built the impressive, three-storey South Tower, complete with battlements. The only access to this stout construction – whose walls are 5ft (1.5m) thick – was via a drawbridge from outside the entrance to the 'solar' room. He also added a defensive curtain wall, topped with battlements, a stone gatehouse,

a drawbridge and an encircling rock-cut moat supplied with water from a large pond just to the south-west. The wall originally stood 34ft (10.3m) high from the bottom of the moat. Yet, although Stokesay Castle had some defensive capability, it was not designed to withstand a serious attack. The Great Hall, for example, was built with large windows facing Wales, the direction from which Lawrence said he feared attack. As in other fortified manor houses, comfort was deemed more important than defence. However, although far from impregnable, Lawrence's fortified manor was certainly sufficiently grand for him to entertain the Bishop of Hereford and his retinue for ten days.

LATER DEVELOPMENTS

Lawrence did not live to enjoy his castle for long, as he drowned in a shipwreck in 1294. Nevertheless, his descendants remained in possession of Stokesay for more than three centuries, and in the 14th and 15th centuries often served as sheriffs of Shropshire. The castle and lands were sold to pay off debts in 1598. In the 1630s, Stokesay

was let on a long lease to Charles Baldwyn, MP for Ludlow, who replaced the original stone gatehouse with a charming half-timbered building, which still survives. In the Civil War, Stokesay's then owner, Lord Craven, declared for the king, but surrendered to a parliamentary army in 1645 before any damage was done to the 'castle'. In line with their normal policy of slighting fortified defences, the Parliamentarians reduced the height of the curtain wall.

UNUSUAL ATTRIBUTES

Stokesay Castle is notable as one of the earliest English stone houses. It was built of local Silurian limestone, quarried just across the valley. Unless good-quality building stone was available locally, as here or in the Cotswolds, building in stone in this period was prohibitively expensive for all but the wealthiest landowners because it involved not only quarrying but also transporting the very heavy material over great distances. Generally, it was only the king, his leading barons and churchmen who could meet the necessary cost.

Stokesay Castle is also highly unusual in that its central buildings survive largely unaltered from the time of Lawrence of

Below: The solar chamber in the South Tower was warmed by sunlight through the large windows and the fire of its chimneypiece.

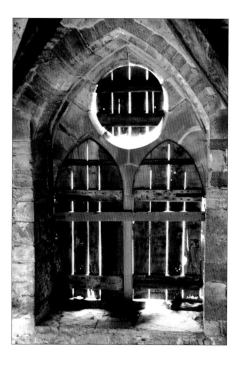

Above: The gabled windows in the Great Hall were part-glazed: the upper part and the circular 'eye' above were glazed; the lower part was closed with shutters in the cold.

Ludlow in the 13th century. The buildings were unoccupied after 1706, and so were not altered in line with prevailing fashions. After 150 years, during which Stokesay fell gradually into picturesque ruins, and was used by a nearby farm, the 'castle' was bought and restored by Victorian philanthropist and glove-manufacturer J.D. Allcroft. It was further repaired in the 1980s and has been held by English Heritage since 1992.

PENSHURST PLACE
HOME OF SIR PHILIP SIDNEY

Penshurst Place in Kent is one of England's earliest and finest fortified manor houses. Celebrated above all for its later association with Renaissance poet and soldier, Sir Philip Sidney, and the Sidney family, Penshurst began life as a 13th-century house owned by Sir Stephen de Penchester (d.1299). In c.1340, Sir John de Poulteney, four times Lord Mayor of London, transformed the house into a country mansion where, within a day's ride of the capital, he could entertain and hunt.

HALL AND 'SOLAR'

The magnificent Barons' Hall, with a 60ft (18m) high roof made of chestnut wood and large octagonal central hearth, was completed in 1341. In this cavernous, smoky chamber, Sir John's servants ate and slept. Vast trestle-mounted wooden tables were used: the two wooden tables at Penshurst are 13th-century originals,

the only surviving examples of their kind in England. As at Stokesay and in other medieval halls, the smoke rose to the ceiling to escape through smoke louvers or slatted openings.

Three Gothic screens disguise the passage to the kitchen and offices. A stone staircase leads up to the house's state apartments. The first was originally a 'solar room'. It subsequently became an ante-room (reception area) in the Elizabethan era and, later still, the State Dining Room. (In 1430, Henry V's brother, John, Duke of Bedford, built a second hall to the south-west of the solar block adjoining the original Barons' Hall. The new hall, now called the Buckingham Building, had mullioned windows added in the 16th century.)

A FORTIFIED MANOR

In c.1390, amid fears of a French invasion, the owner of Penshurst Place was granted a licence to crenellate, and fortified the

Above: Sir Philip Sidney served Elizabeth I and knew many other great figures of the age, including Sir Walter Raleigh.

Below: From the ornate fountain in the Italian Garden at Penshurst Place there is a splendid view of the south front of the house.

Left: The Long Gallery at Penshurst (1601) was typical of those added to country houses in Elizabeth I's reign.

mansion with a curtain wall containing eight defensive towers. As at Stokesay, the house was sufficiently well fortified to repel a minor assault, but a well-armed army would have had little difficulty in gaining entry. Today, the bulk of these fortifications have gone. Some were dismantled and others used as part of later extensions, but one tower remains, standing alongside a stretch of wall in the gardens to the south of the main house.

CROWN PROPERTY

In the late 15th and early 16th century, three dukes of Buckingham owned Penshurst, and all were beheaded. The third was Edward Stafford, who was executed on 17 May 1521, having been found guilty of high treason, supposedly for plotting the king's death and his own elevation to the throne.

As the property of a traitor, the estate was forfeit to the Crown. Penshurst Place came into royal hands, and Henry VIII stayed there when paying court to Anne Boleyn at Hever Castle nearby.

THE SIDNEY FAMILY

Edward VI granted the house and estate to the Sidney family in 1552. Sir Henry Sidney (1529–86) erected a new range and gatehouse to the north of the Barons' Hall. This included an arcade with Tuscan columns, completed in 1579 and perhaps England's earliest classical loggia.

This new building incorporated one of the 14th-century defensive towers; the arcade was later glazed. Sir Henry also created magnificent gardens around the house.

Sir Henry Sidney, whose father was tutor to the future Edward VI, was a childhood friend of the king and grew up at court. He became a trusted servant of the Crown, serving both Mary I and Elizabeth I with distinction, and naming his own son, the celebrated Sir Philip Sidney, after Mary's husband, Philip II of Spain, who was the boy's godfather. Sir Henry's wife, Mary Dudley, was the sister of Queen Elizabeth I's favourite, Robert Dudley, Earl of Leicester. Elizabeth often visited Sir Henry's

home, and the Queen Elizabeth Room, in which she held court when in residence there, is named in her honour.

Sir Philip Sidney, poet, soldier and courtier, author of *Arcadia* and *Defence of Poetry*, was born at Penshurst Place on 30 November 1554. After his death in a military encounter in the Netherlands at the early age of 31, he was given a state funeral in St Paul's Cathedral, becoming the first commoner to be accorded this honour (Nelson was next, in 1805). Sir Philip's brother, Sir Robert, inherited the house and built the Long Gallery, completed in 1601, as an extension to the staterooms. Lit by mullioned windows on both sides, it has elegant oak wainscoting and houses today, as in the early 17th century, many portraits of Sidney family members.

The house still remains in the hands of the Sidney family. Later owners have continued to modify the house, in particular remodelling the staterooms. In the second half of the 20th century, William Sidney, 1st Viscount De l'Isle, lovingly restored the house and estate.

Below: Penshurst's lavish Queen Elizabeth room. The Queen's great favourite, Leicester, was Sir Philip Sidney's uncle.

LEEDS CASTLE
A GIFT FOR QUEEN MARGARET

The full defensive potential of Leeds Castle in Kent was realized only in the late 13th century, when the River Len was dammed to form an artificial lake. By then, Leeds, a royal castle, had been standing on the site for about 200 years.

Before it was dammed, the Len naturally widened at this spot around two small islands. This caught the eye of a minister at the court of King Ethelbert IV of Kent, named Leede. After the Norman Conquest, William I granted the lands to Hamon de Crèvecoeur, whose son Robert built the first stone castle, which took the form of a keep and a gatehouse. Part of a cellar and some of the Gloriette Tower on the smaller northern island survive from this time.

Leeds Castle remained in the hands of the Crèvecoeur family until 1265, when the castle-builder's great-grandson was dispossessed after siding with the rebel baron, Simon de Montfort. Henry III then made a gift of the castle to Roger de Leyburn, whose son William sold it back to the Crown in 1298 to clear debts.

Below: Leeds Castle was much altered in the Tudor era, but some parts date back to the time of the Norman Robert de Crèvecoeur.

A CASTLE FOR QUEENS
Edward I and his first queen, Eleanor, loved the castle and often stayed there. He built a new curtain wall around the larger island, rebuilt the gatehouse on the northern island and added a chapel in the Gloriette Tower.

When Edward I remarried in 1299, he spent his honeymoon at Leeds Castle and then gave the beautifully situated fortress-palace to his new wife, Margaret of France. Their son, Edward II, by

Above: Busts of Henry VIII and his three children, Mary I, Elizabeth I and Edward VI, are on display in the Queen's Gallery.

contrast, gave the castle to a leading courtier – Bartholomew de Badlesmere – who, in 1321, earned the king's wrath when his wife refused to allow Queen Isabella access to the castle. Edward besieged and took the castle, threw Lady Badlesmere in jail and subsequently beheaded Bartholomew.

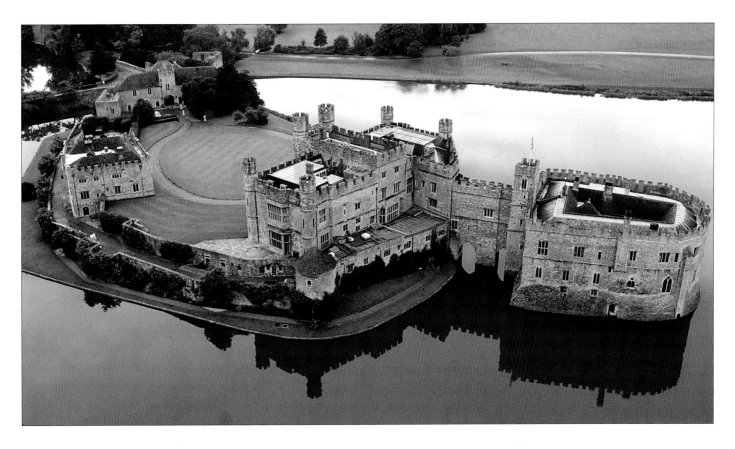

Edward III also admired the castle, and between 1359 and 1377 was engaged in redecorating the royal apartments in the Gloriette Tower. His son and successor, Richard II, hired master mason Henry Yevele, builder of the nave at Canterbury Cathedral and designer of improvements at Westminster Hall, to carry out buiding work at Leeds Castle. Richard followed the royal tradition by giving the castle to his queen, Anne of Bohemia. He must also have liked the place himself because after her death in 1394 he spent a good deal of time there. In 1395, Richard received the French chronicler Jean Froissart at the castle.

Henry Bolingbroke, who deposed Richard II in 1399 and ascended the throne as Henry IV, gave Leeds Castle to his queen and second wife, Joan of Navarre. The couple stayed at the castle in 1403 to escape the plague in London.

IN THE HANDS OF THE TUDORS
Following Henry IV's death, Queen Joan was declared forfeit on charges of sorcery. She was confined in Pevensey Castle, and her stepson, Henry V, was

Above: Black swans live on the lake. They were a gift to British leader Sir Winston Churchill, who gave them to the castle.

free to give Leeds Castle to his beautiful French wife, Catherine of Valois. At Leeds Castle, after Henry V's death, Catherine fell in love with and secretly married Owen Tudor, a Welsh squire. After the secret of their marriage was revealed, Queen Catherine retired to a nunnery at Bermondsey, where she died in 1437, but the union with Tudor had far-reaching consequences, for her grandson by Owen, Henry Tudor, would win the crown in the Battle at Bosworth Field in 1485 and occupy the throne as King Henry VII.

The next royal to be associated with Leeds was Henry VIII, who spent lavishly on the place. He retained the fortifications, but his alterations to the royal apartments made Leeds more palace than fortress (see page 101).

CHAPEL ROYAL

When Edward I's beloved Queen Eleanor died in 1290, a grief-stricken Edward provided for mass to be said daily for her soul in the chapel he had added to the Gloriette Tower on the smaller northern island.

This benefaction – known as a chantry – was extended by Edward II, Richard II, Henry VI and Henry VII. The chapel itself was reconsecrated and made a Chapel Royal by the Archbishop of Canterbury, Donald Coggan, in 1978.

Above: The chapel has a serene atmosphere.

RABY CASTLE
STRONGHOLD OF THE NEVILLES

The powerful Neville family built Raby Castle, at Staindrop in Co Durham, in the late 14th century. Their stronghold stands on a place with venerable royal associations, reputedly the site of a palace belonging to Canute (r.1016-35).

The Nevilles were a significant Norman family who fought alongside William the Conqueror at Hastings and were rewarded with lands in the north of England. They acquired the manor of Raby through marriage in the 13th century, when Isabel Neville married the Lord of Raby, Robert FitzMaldred.

Among prominent early Nevilles was Robert Neville, who was killed at the 1319 Battle of Berwick. From 1334, another Neville, Ralph, served the English Crown as Warden of the Scottish Marches – a key position he shared with Henry Percy, 2nd Baron of Alnwick. The Neville and Percy families became fierce competitors for prominence and royal favour.

Below: In the 18th century, when this view of Raby was painted, the Vane family reworked the west wing and entrance hall.

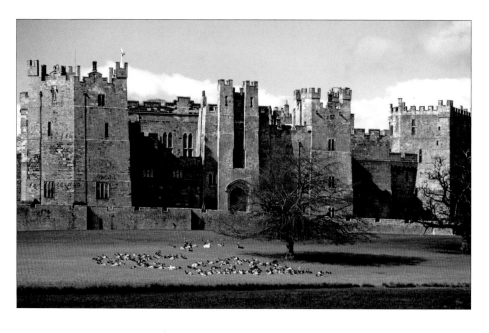

Above: Fortified mansion. Grandeur and comfort outweighed defensive effectiveness in the considerations of the builders at Raby.

NEW DEFENCES

Ralph's son, Sir John Neville, was granted a licence to crenellate and embattle all the towers, houses and walls at Raby by the Bishop of Durham in 1378. By this date the castle was well established, and doubtless fortified, but Sir John added new defences to his family stronghold, so that the castle had the key elements of a defensible fortress, with a moat, drawbridge, gatehouse and curtain wall 30ft (9m) high. But within the inner enclosure, the arrangement of towers and other fortifications was planned not to maximize defensive capabilities, but rather to emphasize both the power and the grandeur of the Neville family.

THE NEVILLE GATEWAY

In the late 14th century, Sir John built the Neville Gateway in the western part of the castle, where the majority of the surviving medieval work is found and some of the walls are 20ft (6m) thick. The gateway is a celebration in stone of the family's ascent to power and pre-eminence: it bears the symbols of the Cross of St George (in reference to Sir John's acceptance as a Knight of the Garter in 1369) alongside the Nevilles' own saltire (St Andrew's cross) and a Latimer cross (because Sir John's second wife, named Elizabeth, was the heiress of the prominent Latimer family of Corby).

The gateway was the sole point of access to the inner court, and was originally fitted with a gate and drawbridge across the moat. From the gateway, a tunnel 70ft (21m) long leads to the inner court. Other elements surviving from the 14th century are the Chapel Tower (although this has an 18th-century doorway), the Servants' Hall and the splendid Kitchen Tower, which is almost entirely unchanged since its construction *c.*1360. The Great Hall may have been begun as early as 1320. Records show that in the mid-14th century, master mason John Lewyn was active at Raby, as he was at nearby Durham Cathedral.

IMPRESSIVE TOWERS

Sir John's son, another Ralph, was an active builder at Raby and at another Neville property, Middleham Castle. In all, at Raby there were two gatehouses (an outer one, in the north, in addition to the inner Neville Gateway) and nine towers. Eight of the towers survive, including the majestic Clifford's Tower, 80ft (24m) in height. However, one in the southerly part of the castle was replaced by a dining room in the 1840s, when the south range was entirely rebuilt. At the south-east corner of the castle is the 11th-century Bulmer's

---

SITE OF CANUTE'S PALACE?

Raby probably stands on the site of a palace belonging to Canute, the 'Emperor of the North' and England's Danish king in 1016–35. The name of the settlement derives from the Danish 'ra' for 'boundary' and 'bi' for homestead. By tradition, Canute gave the estate to the monks of St Cuthbert, and the prior granted the land to Dolfin, a descendant of King Malcolm II of Scots. Dolfin's grandson was Robert Fitzmaldred, who married into the great Norman family of Neville (see main text). The Nevilles built on the association of their castle with Canute by inventing a bloodline showing they were descended from a niece of Canute himself. Raby tradition also claims that the oldest parts of Bulmer's Tower at the castle were built in Canute's time.

Tower, a uniquely unusual five-sided 11th-century building, named after the Norman knight Bertram de Bulmer. The only other tower of this shape is found in Denmark.

LATER ALTERATIONS

The Nevilles fell dramatically from power and influence in 1569, and in the late 16th century, Raby Castle was forfeit to the Crown. In 1626, the castle and estate were bought by Sir Henry Vane, who built an arcade on the courtyard's eastern edge and added a five-bay façade on the central block. In the 18th century, his descendant Gilbert Vane employed the architect James Paine to produce the Hunter's Gallery and remodel the interiors of much of the west wing. In the 1780s, Sir Gilbert's son employed architect John Carr of

Above: In the Barons' Hall at Raby, 700 knights gathered in 1569 to plot the ill-fated Rising of the North against Elizabeth I.

York in the extraordinary project of refashioning the entrance hall so that a coach and horses could pass through it.

The 19th-century alterations by William Burn, a fashionable designer and remodeller of country houses, were unfortunately of the 'improving' early Victorian kind that swept away much that would have been of interest to later generations. In particular, Burn removed medieval vaulting from the Clifford and Bulmer Towers. Yet Raby Castle still makes an undeniably impressive impact, not least because of its size, but also because it retains a large number of authentic architectural elements surviving from the 14th century.

BODIAM CASTLE
CASTLE ON AN ISLAND

 Of all the fortified great houses of the 14th century, Bodiam Castle in East Sussex probably has the best claim to being a truly defensible stronghold. It was clearly a comfortable and splendid dwelling, with elegant and well-designed residential quarters, but it also boasted four strong corner towers, a twin-towered gatehouse and wide water defences with a complex approach designed with defence much in mind.

The castle was built under a licence to crenellate ('for the defences of the adjacent county and the resistance against our enemies') granted to Sir Edward Dakygrigge by Richard II in 1385, at a time when the French had the upper hand in the English Channel, and at the height of English fears of an invasion. Sir Edward's manor of Bodiam stood in the valley of the River Rother, which at that time was large enough to be navigable by sizeable ships as far as Bodiam itself.

FRENCH DESIGN
Sir Edward built his fortified manor house at Bodiam from scratch, having abandoned the existing manor house nearby, which he had acquired through marriage, to create a compact castle. He based the design on continental fortifications he had seen first-hand when fighting in France under the command of Sir Robert Knollys during the reign of Richard II's predecessor and grandfather, King Edward III. The castle was rectangular. Four corner towers 60ft (18m) tall were linked by a defensive wall two storeys high, which included a square tower in the west and east walls, a vast gatehouse facing north and an additional postern tower situated in the south face.

BODIAM'S DEFENCES
The castle is, today, approached along a straight causeway from the north across the moat via a small octagonal island, but originally visitors – or, perhaps more

Above: The view of Bodiam across the moat from the south-east shows the postern tower (left, centre) in the two-storey south wall.

relevantly, attackers – had to approach from the west side of the moat and make a right-angled turn on the small island, all the while leaving themselves vulnerable to attack from the castle. Once on the octagonal island, the approach involved passing across a drawbridge to a barbican tower, then across another drawbridge to the castle's main gatehouse. The gatehouse itself was

---

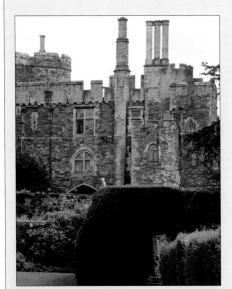

Above: Terraced gardens surround Berkeley Castle. From the gardens there are fine views of the country and the River Severn.

BERKELEY CASTLE'S GREAT HALL
A majestic Great Hall was added to the 12th-century castle at Berkeley in Gloucestershire *c.*1340 by Thomas, 3rd Lord Berkeley. With large windows and a cavernous timbered roof, it stands 62ft (19m) long and 32ft (10m) high. Only 13 years earlier, the castle had been the scene of one of the most infamous events in English royal history: the murder in captivity of King Edward II, on 21 September 1327. Lord Thomas was cleared of responsibility for the deed and is remembered in both the Berkeley family and wider tradition as a man of compassion. However, closer investigation suggests that he must have known of the dark deeds and indeed sent news of the king's death to Queen Isabella and her lover, Roger Mortimer, Earl of March.

Above: A succession of monarchs, from Henry VII and Elizabeeth I to George IV, has been entertained in the Great Hall.

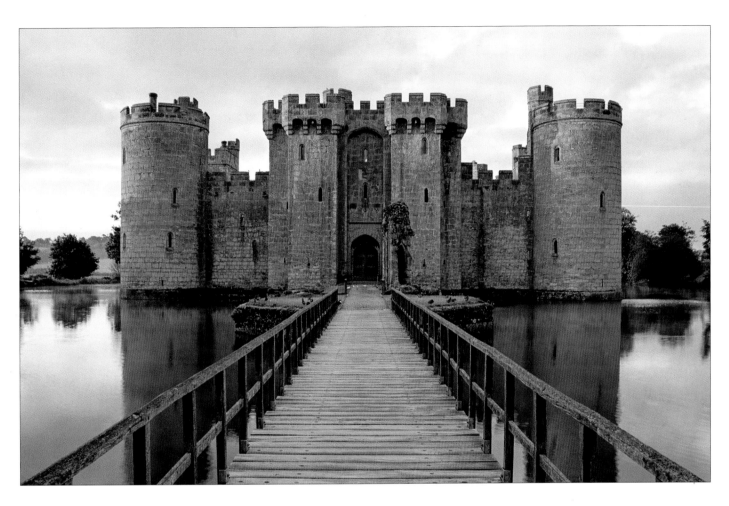

fitted with three portcullises and three gates, as well as gun-holes, and 'murder holes' through which materials could be thrown at or poured down on anyone trying to attack the castle.

The castle came under attack twice. The first occasion was in 1483, when Bodiam's then owner, Sir Thomas Lewknor, had provoked the anger of Richard III. The king sent the Earl of Surrey to seek revenge, and Sir Thomas surrendered his castle without a struggle. Then, in 1643, during the English Civil War, Parliamentarian forces took the castle, again without a fight. The Roundheads left the outer castle intact, but caused severe damage within.

LUXURY WITHIN

Today, the castle's inner buildings remain in ruins, but it is possible to recreate a picture of the luxurious accommodation provided for Sir Edward Dalyngrigge in the 14th century. The public buildings included a large chapel, a Great Hall and a large Public Chamber. Sir Edward's

elegant private chambers were in the east range's first floor and included a hall – complete with crenellated fireplace – giving access to two sleeping chambers, each with a garderobe, situated in the square tower on the castle's east wall. Sir Edward's private hall also gave access to a reserved side-chapel at first-floor level overlooking the altar in the main castle chapel. Thus, Sir Edward and his family could maintain their privacy while joining garrison soldiers at worship in the main chapel below.

RESTORATION DISCOVERIES

The castle at Bodiam was purchased and meticulously restored in the early 20th century by Lord Curzon, one-time Viceroy of India. Another indication of the level of luxury provided in this elegant fortified manor house was that, during restoration, Curzon found evidence of 33 fireplaces and no fewer than 28 lavatories, which were constructed in the curtain wall and gave directly into the moat.

Above: Easy access. On Bodiam's north face, a railed walkway now leads across the moat to the barbican and the gatehouse.

Below: The 60ft (18m) cylindrical corner towers of the four-sided castle at Bodiam each contain four storeys.

WESTMINSTER PALACE
HENRY III'S RESIDENCE

King Henry III (r.1216–72) was one of the greatest of England's royal builders. He spent £10,000 improving Westminster Palace, the royal residence first built alongside the Thames to the east of Westminster Abbey by Edward the Confessor (r.1042–66). Westminster was Edward's favourite palace and, in his time, as a result of his improvements, the finest in Europe (see page 27).

Henry's reign saw the building of the reputedly magnificent King's Great Chamber, or Painted Chamber, which measured 80 x 26ft (24 x 8m) and 31ft (9m) high, with a beautiful timbered ceiling and patterned floor tiles. Its walls were covered with superb murals by Masters William of Westminster and Walter of Durham, showing scenes from the Old Testament and the life of St Edward the Confessor. Nearby, Henry built new apartments for his queen, Eleanor, but these and the Painted Chamber were both destroyed in the fire that devastated the palace in 1834 – only the crypt of St Stephen's Chapel, the Jewel Tower and Westminster Hall, with its magnificent hammerbeam roof, survived the fire.

THE JEWEL TOWER

The three-storey tower was built in 1365–6, probably by master mason Henry Yevele, to store the king's jewels, furs and other valuables. At the extreme southern edge of the palace complex, it was partially surrounded by a moat.

Above: The Jewel Tower is built from Kentish ragstone. Today it houses a collection of local archaeological finds.

It continued to be used as a royal store for valuables until the reign of Henry VII (r.1485–1509).

WINCHESTER PALACE

Winchester Palace, the London home of the Bishop of Winchester, was built in Southwark in 1109. Like Westminster Palace, it was improved in the later medieval period but largely destroyed by fire in the 19th century. The marriage reception for James I of Scots and Joan Beaufort was held there in 1424. Tradition has it Henry VIII met his fifth wife Catherine Howard there in 1540.

Right: The west wall, with its magnificent rose window, c. 1320, is the only part of the Great Hall to survive today.

THE HAMMERBEAM ROOF

The other surviving part of the palace is Westminster Hall, built by William Rufus in 1097. Significant alterations were made to the hall by Richard II from 1394 onward. Following designs by Henry Yevele, the walls were raised 2ft (0.6m) and refaced, and a magnificent hammerbeam roof, by Hugh Herland, was added. The roof, carved with angels and traceries, has a span of 69ft (21m), making it the largest timber roof in northern Europe, and soars to a height of 92ft (28m). Richard also built a gateway to the hall containing carved statues of English kings from Edward the Confessor onward.

EDINBURGH CASTLE
CASTLE ON A ROCK

 During the reign of King David II of Scots (r.1329–71), major rebuilding work took place in Edinburgh Castle (see also page 106). The great volcanic rock on which the castle stands high above the city was a natural place for a fortified dwelling – and archaeologists have found evidence of settlement, as far back as the Bronze Age (2100–700BC). In the Norman era, Malcolm III (r.1058–93) built a stone castle on the rock. His queen, Margaret, died after hearing that Malcolm had been killed in an ambush in Northumbria; King David I (r.1125–53), her son, built the tiny Chapel of St Margaret in her honour in the castle precincts. This small, irregular chapel is the only part of the Norman castle that still survives today.

Below: Edinburgh Castle was a royal palace and military fortress until modern times.

DAVID'S TOWER

In the 14th century, Robert Stewart – grandson of Robert the Bruce, nephew of the reigning King David II, and himself the future King Robert II – built an L-shaped tower on the castle's northern side. Constructed in 1368–72 and almost 60ft (18m) high, the building, subsequently known as 'David's Tower', almost certainly contained royal apartments. Kitchens and offices were built alongside it in 1382–3. David's Tower is the first known example in Scotland of the tower house – a design pioneered by royalty that would become popular among the nobility. Historians cannot be sure of the exact layout of rooms within the tower, but above a vaulted ground floor they probably contained a first-floor suite for the king, comprising hall, private chamber and closet, with a similar suite for the queen on the floor above.

Above: St Margaret's Chapel is the oldest surviving building in Edinburgh. The tiny chapel holds only around 20 people.

The tower survived unscathed for around two centuries, but then its upper floors were destroyed in a 1573 siege during the reign of James VI of Scots, the future James I of England. The surviving part of the tower was then incorporated into the castle's Half Moon Battery, only to be rediscovered in the early 20th century.

IGHTHAM MOTE
A PICTURESQUE MANOR HOUSE

 An idyllic manor house near Sevenoaks in Kent, Ightham Mote is arranged compactly around a courtyard and is enclosed by a stream-fed moat. The house retains a sturdy, well-worn and utilitarian beauty. The earliest buildings, including the massive Great Hall, date from the 14th century, but important additions, including a wonderfully decorated Tudor chapel, were made over the following 200–300 years.

IGHTHAM'S ORIGINS

The house's curious name comes from the nearby village of Ightham and that of the 'moot' (local council), which in medieval times met in the most prominent house in each locality. Its first named owner was Sir Thomas Cawne (d.1374),

Below: A stone urn stands on the lawn in the inner courtyard at Ightham Mote. The buildings behind are called the 'Elizabethan cottages' but in fact date to c.1475.

Right: The south-west front contains the central castellated gatehouse, accessed by a stone bridge across the moat.

who lived in the house from c.1340. The earliest surviving buildings are those on the east side of the courtyard: the Great Hall, the old chapel with crypt, a kitchen and two solars or private chambers. Timber dating indicates that these rooms were completed c.1330, although there is some evidence that the crypt is a survival from an earlier house on the site. The moat and bridge were also laid out in the first half of the 14th century.

In the years 1487–1519, the house's then owner, Edward Haut, added south and west sides to the courtyard. Facing the bridge over the moat, he built a battlemented three-storey entrance tower or gatehouse – the only fortification on the site. On either side of the tower, he built two-storey residential quarters and added a similar two-storey range on the south side of the yard.

TUDOR CHAPEL

In 1521–38, Sir Richard Clement, a notable figure at the court of Henry VIII, left his mark upon the house. Sir Richard added a new chapel on the north side of the courtyard in the form of an upper-floor timber room overhanging the moat with a cloister beneath. This beautiful Gothic chapel was fitted with a delicately carved tracery screen, six fine Dutch stained-glass windows, a hooded pulpit, linen-fold

Built *c*.1300 by Sir John de Broughton, Broughton Castle, near Banbury in Oxfordshire, is another fine example of the 14th-century fortified manor house. The house, protected by a wide moat, can be reached only by a single bridge across the moat and through a gatehouse.

Sir John de Broughton's manor house was sufficiently splendid to catch the eye of William of Wykeham, Chancellor of England and Bishop of Winchester, who purchased the property in 1377. His great-nephew Sir Thomas Wykeham added battlements to the gatehouse under a licence 'to crenellate and embattle' granted in 1406.

The Fiennes family, later Lords Saye and Sele, acquired the manor through marriage to Sir Thomas Wykeham's

Right: Broughton Castle's moat covers 3 acres (1.2ha). The house has a medieval Great Hall and fine plaster ceilings.

BROUGHTON CASTLE

grand-daughter, Margaret, in 1448. In the Tudor period, Broughton Castle was substantially remodelled. During Charles I's reign, William, 8th Lord Saye and Sele, a leading Puritan and supporter of Parliament against the king, used Broughton as a meeting place for the king's opponents.

The family frittered away its wealth during the Regency period, but this had the unlooked-for and fortunate effect of subsequently saving Broughton from the

'improving' hand of Victorian architects. Building work was limited to repairs, begun in 1860 by Frederick, 16th Lord Saye and Sele, and continuing throughout the 20th century.

Broughton has won many admirers over the centuries: novelist Henry James called it 'the most delightful home in England' and it was used as the setting for *Shakespeare in Love* (1998) and *The Madness of King George* (1994).

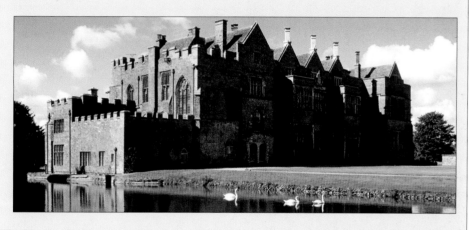

wall panelling and an arched ceiling with panels brightly painted with the Tudor rose, the arrows of Aragon (birthplace of Queen Catherine), the Beaufort portcullis and other emblems.

Below: This carved stone head is from the courtyard at Ightham Mote.

When it was finished, the chapel was somewhat reminiscent of a tournament pavilion of the kind used at events such as the outdoor peace summit, at the Field of the Cloth of Gold in France, organized by Cardinal Wolsey in 1520. Sir Richard also added stained-glass windows to the Great Hall, and window barge boards, once again decorated with Tudor symbols, to the oriel room.

The essential elements that give Ightham Mote its great charm were now in place. In later years, notable owners included Sir William and Dame Dorothy Selby, who, in 1611–41, added the drawing room and the rooms alongside. After 1889, Sir Thomas Colyer-Fergusson carried out widespread repairs.

AMERICAN PHILANTHROPIST

In the second half of the 20th century, the house was saved from possible demolition by an enlightened American businessman, Charles Henry Robinson of Portland, Maine. He purchased

Ightham Mote and funded its renovation from afar, staying in the house during his visits to Europe. Upon his death in 1985, he left the house to the National Trust.

Below: There is a heraldic crest above the main entrance to Ightham Mote.

CHAPTER FOUR

CASTLES AND MANOR HOUSES

1400–1485

Sir Edward Bedingfeld began building the fortified manor house of Oxburgh Hall, near King's Lynn in Norfolk, under a licence to crenellate granted by Edward IV in 1482. The house's elegant design and the superb brickwork of its imposing twin-towered gatehouse make a very grand impression. Auguste Pugin called the house 'one of the noblest expressions of the domestic architecture of the 15th century'. This was a period that saw the rise of the brick-built tower and fortified house. Brick began to replace stone at a time when 'castles' were, in fact, houses built in the style of fortresses, and did not have to be defensible against siege engines. The great appeal of bricks was that they made possible details of surface patterning that could not be produced in stone; they were also cheaper than dressed stone and could be made on site.

One of the pioneers of the brick-built tower was the soldier and courtier, Sir John Falstaff, who began the splendid Caister Castle, in Norfolk, in 1432. At around the same time, Sir John's old friend and companion-at-arms, Ralph, Lord Cromwell, Treasurer of England under King Henry VI, erected a superb brick tower at Tattershall Castle, Lincolnshire. A decade later, another prominent figure at King Henry VI's court, Sir Roger de Fiennes, also Treasurer of the King's Household, began work on the elegant brick-built country house of Herstmonceux Castle in East Sussex. Then, later in the century, Sir John Wenlock rebuilt in brick at Someries Castle in Bedfordshire in the 1460s, and Thomas Rotherham, Bishop of Lincoln, commissioned a fine brick palace at Buckden, Huntingdonshire, in the 1470s.

Left: Castle in brick. Henry VI's treasurer, Sir Roger de Fiennes, spared no expense on his country mansion of Herstmonceux Castle, spending £3,800 on its construction.

TATTERSHALL CASTLE
SPLENDID BRICKWORK

Tattershall Castle was, like Bodiam Castle in Sussex, purchased and renovated by Lord Curzon of Kedleston upon his return from service as Viceroy of India. In the case of Tattershall, Curzon's intervention was very timely because when he bought the property, in 1910, its four superb carved-stone fireplaces had been taken out of the brickwork tower and were packed in boxes in London, waiting to be shipped to the United States. Lord Curzon reinstalled the fireplaces and devotedly refurbished the castle, which he declared 'the most splendid piece of brickwork in England'.

THE GREAT TOWER

The magnificent surviving Great Tower at Tattershall was erected by Ralph, Lord Cromwell, in 1432–8, as part of improvements to an earlier castle built *c.*1231 by Robert of Tattershall.

A prominent figure at court, Cromwell served as an adviser to Henry V before he was appointed Treasurer of England by Henry VI in 1433. At Tattershall, he clearly set out to build a lordly dwelling that befitted his newly won eminence.

Cromwell spared no expense to make his mark: his tower, which rose 100ft (30m) above the flat Lincolnshire countryside, was built using costly small red bricks, which were becoming increasingly fashionable. In the tower and nearby buildings at the castle, Cromwell's builders used one million bricks made in his local kilns.

Left: Both inside and out at Tattershall, Cromwell's Flemish and French craftsmen produced brickwork of the highest quality.

Above: Putting elegance and comfort before defence, Tattershall Castle contains sizeable windows fitted with heraldic stained glass.

The tower was not a military stronghold: it had ornate traceried windows and no fewer than three doors at ground level, and the corner turrets at parapet level were not defensively functional, since they were covered by mini-spires. In fact, it was designed for grandeur and comfort. It contained a vaulted basement beneath four residential floors, each of which held a great central hall with additional rooms and garderobes in the thick walls and the corner towers. On the ground floor was a Courtroom or Parlour, its carved stone fireplace beautifully decorated with heraldic devices of Cromwell's family. The first floor contained a Great Hall; the second provided an Audience Chamber and ceremonial area with magnificent moulded brick vaulting; and the third was the Lord's Privy Chamber or bedchamber.

Throughout, the castle, brickwork and stone carving were exquisitely finished, and, thanks to Lord Curzon's initiative in renovating and refurbishing the castle, these features can be seen and appreciated today.

DEFENCES

Ralph Cromwell lavished money on the comfort and appearance of his show-piece tower, but he did not entirely neglect the castle's overall defences. He added an outer moat to the building complex and constructed no fewer than three gatehouses and three bridges to guard the approach to the castle from the north.

Cromwell probably repaired and strengthened the 13th-century inner curtain wall, which contained eight drum towers and enclosed in the inner ward a separate Great Hall, as well as kitchens and a chapel. Little remains today except the superb tower.

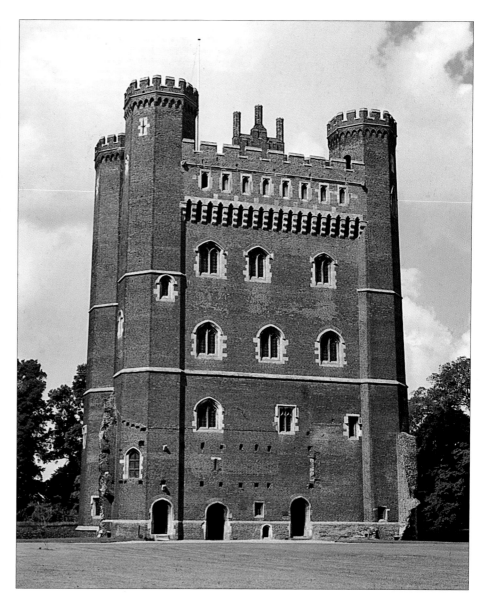

Above: From the cellars to the battlements, there are no fewer than six floors in the great Square Keep at Tattershall Castle.

CAISTER CASTLE, NORFOLK

Sir John Falstaff, a veteran of the Battle of Agincourt and Henry V's military campaigns in France, and subsequently Governor of Maine and Anjou, rebuilt his family home at Caister, in Norfolk, in some style in 1432–46. His 'castle' was a rectangular brick country house, as lavishly fitted and furnished as a palace. The English chronicler William Worcester described it as a 'ryche juelle' ('rich jewel'). But it was also fortified and surrounded by a moat. It originally had four corner towers, but only one remains, an impressive five storeys, 100ft (30m) in height. Although the tower has machicolations and gun-holes, its large windows would have made it difficult to defend against a besieging force.

Right: The builder of Caister Castle is thought to have been Shakespeare's model for the character of Sir John Falstaff.

RETURN TO THE SQUARE KEEP

Architectural historians note that the square keep was not commonly built in England at the time of Lord Cromwell – the great English square keeps at the Tower of London, at Colchester and Rochester had been constructed three centuries earlier. They suggest that Cromwell may have been inspired to build in this way by the contemporary square keeps he saw in France, when on campaign with the English Army. The quality and style of the workmanship suggests that he imported the finest craftsmen from Flanders and France to work on the building.

LINLITHGOW PALACE
HOME OF THE SCOTTISH KINGS

 King James I of Scots began the extensive rebuilding of the royal palace at Linlithgow, between Edinburgh and Stirling, in 1424. In that year, James returned to Scotland, aged 30, at the end of a prolonged 18-year exile in England that had begun when he was captured by pirates, while travelling to France, and handed over to England's King Henry IV. Under the terms of his release treaty, signed in 1423 with England's new king, Henry VI, James had to pay a ransom of £40,000. Nevertheless, James still found the necessary funds to undertake the reconstruction of Linlithgow, where a terrible fire a year later had devastated the earlier fortified dwelling.

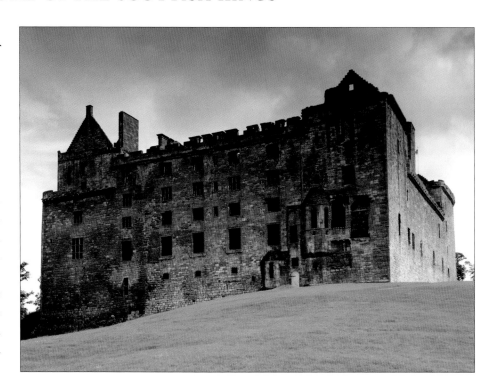

QUEENS AND KINGS AT LINLITHGOW

According to Scottish royal tradition, in June 1513 Queen Margaret (Tudor), English-born wife of James IV, waited at Linlithgow for her royal husband to return from the Battle of Flodden Field, unaware that he lay dead with 10,000 of his fellow countrymen. The castle's north-west tower, in which she is said to have waited, is named Queen Margaret's Bower in her honour.

Later, Mary, Queen of Scots, was born at Linlithgow in December 1542, and after she returned to the Scottish throne following her long French exile she often stayed at the palace. Subsequently, Linlithgow began to become neglected, although Charles I stayed there in 1617 and again in 1633.

In 1745, Bonnie Prince Charlie stayed at the palace prior to his unsuccessful attempt to march on London. Subsequently, the Duke of Cumberland (son of England's King George II) stayed there with his army. When these troops departed on 1 February 1746, a fire left unattended started a devastating blaze that severely damaged the palace. Significant repairs were carried out in the 19th century.

Left: Mary, Queen of Scots, spent the first seven months of her life at Linlithgow Palace and often returned afterwards.

Above: The Renaissance-style north façade at Linlithgow was built by James VI and may have been based on the Chateau de Blois in the Loire Valley, France.

FIRST ROYAL BUILDING

King David I of Scots was the earliest royal builder at Linlithgow, erecting a manor house of timber in the mid-12th century. When Edward I of England invaded in the late 13th century, he and his trusted castle architect, Master James of St Georges, fortified David's palace with earthworks, ditches and wooden palisades, but stopped short of building in stone. Edward garrisoned the castle with the English troops needed for his Scottish campaigns. Subsequently, David II carried out rebuilding in the 14th century, but his work was swept away by the fire of 1424.

JAMES I'S CONTRIBUTION

James built an impressive stone entrance block on the east side of the surviving palace building. The raised entranceway was accessed by a ramp and drawbridge from the outer barbican. Above the entrance was the royal coat of arms and on either side were niches, believed once to have held statues of St Andrew and St James. The block also contained a first-floor Great Hall, measuring 100 x 30ft (30 x 9m). At one end were the royal kitchens, while at the other, perhaps, was a great stone fireplace, although in James's time there may have been a great chimneyless central hearth, as in English medieval halls such as Penshurst Place and Stokesay Castle.

The finished palace at Linlithgow took the form of a courtyard house, with four 'wings' around a central garden containing a fountain. Only the eastern front and part of the southern range were finished by James I, but there is evidence that the palace's courtyard was part of the plans from the start. Scholars believe that James, who was an accomplished artist as well as a learned man, may have played a significant part in designing Linlithgow himself. His project

Below: The courtyard fountain of c.1538. James V's queen, Mary of Guise, likened the palace to the best French chateaux.

was never finished, but it appears to have been conceived as a palace, a royal dwelling, rather than a castle. James changed the entrance from the south to the east, constructing a very grand raised but unfortified gateway that could be viewed advantageously from that direction, across the waters of the adjacent

Above: The palace stands beside Linlithgow Loch. This reconstruction shows the complex shortly after its completion by James V.

Loch Linlithgow. The palace may have been planned as the Scottish answer to England's Sheen Palace, which James must certainly have visited during his long exile in England.

THE PLAN COMPLETED

In the 15th and early 16th centuries, Kings James III and IV finished the work begun by James I, enclosing the courtyard by completing the southern range and then building on the north and finally the west sides. The west range contained some splendid royal apartments for James IV and his English queen, Margaret Tudor, daughter of Henry VII. James IV also made repairs and improvements to the Great Hall, to which he added a new roof, and built a new chapel.

In the time of James V, the main entrance was moved back to the southern range, and a new gatehouse built alongside it. James VI then made improvements to the northern range, including the addition of a fine Renaissance façade on the Long Gallery in 1618–24.

RAGLAN CASTLE
THE GRANDEST CASTLE IN WALES

The castle we see at Raglan was begun *c.*1430 by William ap Thomas, veteran of the Battle of Agincourt and later celebrated as 'the Blue Knight of Gwent', following his knighting by King Henry VI in 1449. William built the hexagonal keep known as the Yellow Tower of Gwent (*c.*1435-45), generally celebrated as being among the finest towers of the 15th century.

The Blue Knight was a follower of Richard, Duke of York, and his family's rise was accelerated by the success of the Yorkists, and in particular by Edward of York's coming to the throne as King Edward IV in 1461. By this time Sir William had died, but his son, another Sir William, was made Earl of Pembroke and Chief Justice first of South Wales, then of North Wales too. The younger Sir William completed the castle.

NORMAN CASTLE
Little remains of the early 12th-century motte-and-bailey castle that was built by followers of William FitzOsbern, Earl

Below: The Closet Tower stands to the right of the Great Gatehouse and contained a basement prison. The gatehouse, with its half-hexagonal towers, dates to the 1460s.

of Hereford, as the Normans pushed into Gwent. But it is likely that the Yellow Tower stands on what was the motte, or mound, of the Norman castle and that the castle's two enclosures, the Pitched Stone Court and the Fountain Court, occupy the land that was once the Norman castle's bailey.

YELLOW TOWER
The Yellow Tower of Gwent, so-called because it is made from a pale yellowish sandstone quarried locally at Redbrooke, has walls 10ft (3m) thick. It originally had four floors above the basement, but one level was lost when the castle was slighted in 1646 during the Civil War. Its ground-floor kitchen lay beneath a first-floor hall, which was surmounted by private and sleeping chambers on the levels above.

The tower was surrounded by an apron wall and a wide moat, and accessed only by a single drawbridge from the rest of the castle. It was a formidable stronghold in its own right, and certainly offered secure quarters to which the castle's defenders might retreat *in extremis.* Moreover, in an era of 'bastard feudalism', soldiers and retainers were bound to powerful lords by financial links rather than the ties of

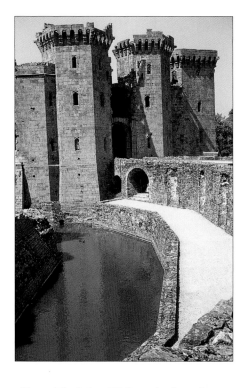

Above: The Moat Walk at the foot of the Yellow Tower was added c.1600 by the Earl of Worcester. Niches in the wall once held statues of Roman emperors.

feudal loyalty, and the lords could not always be sure of the loyalty of the men they used to garrison them. As a result, they often fortified their own quarters within the castle, where they could, if the situation demanded, take refuge from their own garrison.

MACHICOLATION
The gatehouse at Raglan Castle included machicolation – a feature more commonly found in French than Welsh castles. A machicolated defensive wall has a projecting section with holes in the floor through which the castle's defenders could throw rocks or pour oil on attackers. Strictly speaking, the term 'machicolation' refers to the floor opening itself, which was usually between the corbels or supports of the projecting section of wall.

The younger Sir William was responsible for building the splendid Great Hall and accommodation ranged around the Fountain Court, which at one time contained a marble water fountain known

Below: At the top of the Great Gatehouse towers the machicolations can be seen. The windows are narrow for purposes of defence.

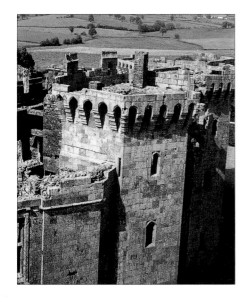

as 'the White Horse'. The retainers' area was in a second courtyard, the Pitched Stone Court, further north.

STRONG DEFENCES

Raglan is an exception to the general movement away from castles to fortified country houses, for it was designed as a fortress proper – one of the last genuine castles ever built. In addition to the Great Tower, it has a curtain wall containing hexagonal towers and a machicolated gatehouse, which was fortified with three heavy double doors, two portcullises and a drawbridge. Throughout the castle, circular gun-ports were provided in the towers to strengthen defences.

In the Elizabethan era, William Somerset, Earl of Worcester, improved the Great Hall. Building in fine red sandstone that makes an appealing contrast to the prevailing yellow stone, he and his descendants carried out significant rebuilding, adding a magnificent Tudor Long Gallery, now ruined.

Above: This aerial view shows the Yellow Tower (near left), the Fountain Court (top left), and the Pitched Stone Court (top right) behind the Great Gatehouse.

CIVIL WAR

Edward Somerset, Marquis of Worcester, was a staunch Royalist, and the castle was the first to be fortified for Charles I during the Civil War. It was a major royalist centre during the war and the last castle to be surrendered to the Parliamentary army. The worth of Raglan's defences was proved by the fact that the surrender took place, in the lavish Great Hall, on 19 August 1646, only after several weeks of heavy bombardment, at the end of one of the war's longest sieges. The victorious Parliamentarians looted and plundered the splendid castle, slighted its defences and partially demolished the Yellow Tower. Raglan Castle has never been restored, and today remains a handsome, evocative ruin.

ST GEORGE'S CHAPEL
AND WINDSOR CASTLE

The magnificent St George's Chapel at Windsor Castle in Berkshire was begun by Edward IV in 1477. By then, Windsor had been a royal stronghold for over 400 years (see pages 153 and 224).

King Edward the Confessor held his court in his palace of Kingsbury at Old Windsor nearby, but after the Conquest William I built the original Windsor

Below: The Choir in St George's Chapel. The banners of the knights of the garter hang above the garter stalls; beneath the banners are the knights' crests, helmets and swords.

Castle, a motte-and-bailey fortification in a strong position on an escarpment overlooking the River Thames. He raised a wooden keep where the Round Tower stands today, atop a 50ft (15m) motte, and enclosed a 13-acre (5ha) bailey with stakes in a boomerang shape.

A ROYAL FAVOURITE

William II chose the castle for his Easter celebrations in 1097; Henry I built a chapel and royal apartments there and married his second wife, Adeliza of Louvain, at Windsor in January 1121. In the 1170s, Henry II rebuilt William I's

Above: St George's Chapel is widely considered to be one of Europe's finest late medieval buildings.

original keep in stone, then reworked the defensive walls around the wards, adding square towers, and refashioned the royal apartments in the upper ward.

In 1216, the fortifications were fully tested when a baronial army besieged King John in the castle for three months. Although the castle held firm, Henry III added three round towers to the western wall. He also established St Edward's Chapel in the lower ward.

Edward III was born in Windsor Castle, in November 1312, and known as 'Edward Windsor'. In the 1360s, he extended and improved the castle, in particular building St George's Hall for the Knights of the Order of the Garter.

ST GEORGE'S CHAPEL

Edward IV began the construction of a vast new chapel dedicated to St George, situated to the west of the earlier one. Master mason Henry Janyns carried out the project, overseen by Richard Beauchamp, Bishop of Salisbury. It was to contain the King's funerary monument. The chapel was unfinished at Edward's death in 1483, and work soon stopped.

The chapel was completed in the reign of Henry VII and became a burial place for British monarchs. No fewer than ten kings and queens are buried there.

NORTON CONYERS
THE HOUSE THAT INSPIRED *JANE EYRE*

Norton Conyers, a fine manor house near Ripon in Yorkshire, was developed by the Conyers, a Norman family granted land in the region after the Conquest of 1066. The house took its present form in the late 1400s, although the Dutch gables and carved doorway on the front are 17th century; the 15th-century brickwork is concealed by an 18th-century roughcast exterior. Norton Conyers appears to have been the inspiration for Thornfield Hall, Mr Rochester's house in Charlotte Brontë's novel *Jane Eyre*.

THE MAD WOMAN IN THE ATTIC

In 1839, when Charlotte Brontë was working as a governess for a family in Harrogate, she visited Norton Conyers and heard her host's account of how, in the 18th century, a mad woman had been locked away in the attic. In her novel *Jane Eyre*, published in 1847, Norton Conyers became Thornfield Hall and the mad woman the wife of the novel's Byronic hero, Mr Rochester.

Below: Charlotte Brontë. In 2004, just as described in Jane Eyre, *a blocked staircase was found at Norton Conyers.*

Norton Conyers stands in a landscaped garden enclosed by a grey stone boundary wall. Within, the impressive Great Hall dates from the 15th century, although its roof timbers have been hidden by a coved ceiling and the original wooden screens have been removed. Norton Conyers also boasts a magnificent 16th-century inlaid table in the hall.

CATHOLIC LORD DISPOSSESSED
The house takes the first part of its name from that of the Norton family, who came into ownership through marriage *c*.1370. However, Richard Norton cast his lot with the Catholic earls who plotted against Elizabeth I at Raby Castle, County Durham, in the doomed 1569 'Rebellion of the North'. As a traitor, Norton lost his property, which was forfeit to the Crown.

THE GRAHAMS TAKE OVER
Norton Conyers was later purchased by Sir Richard Graham, a member of the notable Scots Borders family, in 1624.

Right: The main oak staircase at Norton Conyers, built c.1630, showing some of the Graham portrait collection.

Above: Generations of prosperity. Tudor, Stuart and Georgian additions to the original 14th-century house take nothing away from the charm of Norton Conyers.

In 1644, family legend has it that a wounded Graham horseman rode back so fast from the Battle of Marston Moor that when he reached home his horse's hooves were red-hot. The animal carried its rider into the house because he was wounded, and left a hoof mark on the sweeping oak staircase of *c*.1630.

In 1679, the Grahams entertained the future King James II, then James, Duke of York, with his wife, Mary of Modena, on their way to Scotland. Sir Richard's descendants still own the house today.

OXBURGH HALL
A ROMANTIC MOATED MANOR

Oxburgh Hall has stylish defences – it lies within a square moat and has a gatehouse tower complete with battlements, arrow-slits and machicolations – but, as with many fortified manor houses, these features are more signs of status than effective elements of defence. For one thing, the moat is crossed by a fixed bridge rather than a drawbridge; for another, the arrow-slit arrangement means that defenders could not have provided effective cover fire from them. Moreover, the gate-tower has large windows. In addition, the Great Hall, even if sufficiently fortified to deter bands of marauders in the lawless late 15th century, would not repel well-equipped soldiers or withstand a siege.

The house, near King's Lynn in Norfolk, was begun in the 1480s by prominent nobleman, Sir Edward Bedingfeld, descendant of an originally Norman family. Sir Edward's ancestor, Sir Peter Bedingfeld, fought with honour alongside the Black Prince and King Edward III at the Battle of Crécy in 1346.

Below: In addition to its superb brickwork and royal connections, Oxburgh Hall is celebrated for its French parterre gardens.

The fixed bridge across the moat leads through the arched entranceway at the foot of the tower into a central courtyard. Originally, the Great Hall stood on the south side of the courtyard, directly across from the tower, with two-storey residential buildings on the other sides. The Great Hall was demolished by Sir Richard Bedingfeld in 1775 to open up the courtyard to the moat and countryside beyond. Subsequently, two squat towers were raised at the south-west and south-east corners of the courtyard, filling part of the south side.

Above: The fixed bridge across the moat and Oxburgh Hall's twin-towered gatehouse can be seen at the left side of the picture.

THE GATEHOUSE

The two towers of the gatehouse at Oxburgh Hall are topped with serrated battlements and decorated with horizontal brick mouldings. Within the gatehouse, a splendid brick-built spiral stairway rises from the ground-floor armoury to the roof. The first-floor chamber is known as the King's Room because it was occupied by King Henry VII when he visited Oxburgh in 1487. In a small side room on this floor are embroidered wall-hangings sewn by Mary, Queen of Scots, during her long captivity in England. She was assisted in this work by Bess of Hardwick (builder of Hardwick Hall). The second-floor chamber is named the Queen's Room.

During the reign of Mary I, Sir Henry Bedingfeld was in charge of keeping Princess Elizabeth, the future Elizabeth I, in custody, first in the Tower of London, and then under house arrest at Woodstock. However, Elizabeth showed that she bore no grudge to the family by visiting Oxburgh Hall in 1578.

HERSTMONCEUX CASTLE
FORMER HOME OF THE ROYAL OBSERVATORY

 Sir Roger de Fiennes, Treasurer of the King's Household under King Henry VI, began building the vast and magnificent fortified manor house of Herstmonceux Castle, in East Sussex, in 1441. Along with Lord Cromwell of Tattershall Castle and Sir John Falstaff of Caister Castle, de Fiennes was a pioneer of brick building in 15th-century England. At Herstmonceux, he used Flemish brick and probably Flemish craftsmen to erect a handsome moated country mansion.

The place took its name from 12th-century English noblewoman, Idonea de Herst, and her Norman lord, Ingelram de Monceux. Situated just a few miles from the site of the Battle of Hastings, Herstmonceux was a place of note many centuries before Sir Roger began building there.

Below: According to local legend, the lands besides the moat at Herstmonceux are haunted by a lady in white, who is said to have been seduced, then killed, by Sir Roger.

STYLISTIC DEFENCES
The castle is rectangular in shape, with a polygonal (many-sided) tower at each corner, plus smaller towers spaced out along the length of the walls, and an impressive twin-towered gatehouse, 84ft (25.5m) high, boasting a double row of battlements and heavy machicolation. The gatehouse towers are fitted with gun-holes at ground level and arrow-slits further up. However, the castle was built for comfort and elegance, not as a fortress: the brick walls were far too soft and thin to withstand bombardment, and the turrets, machicolation, moat and battlements are for style, not for defence.

FROM PRIVATE TO PUBLIC
Sir Richard de Fiennes, son of Sir Roger, became Baron Dacre in 1458. The house later passed to the Lennard family through marriage. Then, in the 17th century, Thomas Lennard, 15th Lord Dacre, was made Earl of Sussex by King Charles II and married Anne, Duchess of Cleveland. He frittered away the family money, and the castle was sold.

Above: Sir Roger de Fiennes' arms are carved in stone above the arch in the splendid 84ft (25.5m) gatehouse.

A later owner, Robert Hare, dismantled much of the castle's interior and used the bricks from it in rebuilding Herstmonceux Place, a nearby house. The castle was rescued and renovated by Lt-Col Claude Lowther in the early 20th century. He rebuilt the south front in 1911–12. In 1948–88, the castle was the base of the Royal Greenwich Observatory, but later it was turned into an international study centre by the Queen's University, Canada.

HADDON HALL
HOME TO THE 'KING OF THE PEAK'

The handsome medieval manor house of Haddon Hall, near Bakewell in Derbyshire, has a splendid late 15th-century Dining Room and Great Chamber, both with fine original ceiling paintings. In addition, the house and estate contain a 14th-century Banqueting Hall and largely unchanged adjacent kitchens, Jacobean Long Gallery and terraced Elizabethan gardens. Much of Haddon Hall's charm and interest lie in the fact that it was uninhabited – and so unchanged – for around 200 years after the early 1700s, when the owners (from the 16th century, the dukes of Rutland) removed to their other, grander, house at Belvoir Castle. Then, in 1924, the Marquis of Granby, subsequently the 9th Duke, began a sensitive and careful restoration of the house of his ancestors.

Below: Sparse furnishings, richly carved wood panelling and fine plasterwork ceilings typify the rooms at Haddon Hall.

Above: Henry VII celebrates his marriage to Elizabeth of York. The royal couple are carved in the panelling of the dining room.

Haddon Hall stands in the Peak District National Park, on a hill overlooking the River Wye, on land granted by William the Conqueror to an illegitimate son named William Peverel. The oldest parts of the house, including sections of the boundary wall, the lower part of Peverel's Tower and the font and

arches of the Chapel, date from the Norman period. The boundary wall was built under a licence of 1190, which forbade the use of crenellation and stated that the wall should be no more then 12ft (3.7m) high. The battlements on the walls and towers were added later.

BANQUETING HALL

This hall was built *c.*1370, and two windows and two gargoyles survive from the time of its construction. The oak screen and gallery are 15th century, and while the timber roof is a 20th-century one, it is a very skilful addition. Hanging in the hall is a tapestry of *c.*1470, of French *mille fleurs* design with the arms of England, which is believed to have been a gift from King Henry VIII. The kitchens alongside are fitted with well-used, centuries-old equipment, including a chopping block and a salting box.

MURALS AND MEDALLIONS

In the 15th century, fine murals were painted in the chapel: two of St Nicholas, one of St Anne and one of St Christopher carrying the Christ child across a river full of fish. These were

Below: The terraced gardens run down to the River Wye. They were restored in the 1920s to their appearance in Elizabethan times.

Above: A 15th-century mural in the chapel shows Saint Christopher's feet treading river waters as he carries the Christ child.

Right: Light floods into Haddon Hall's splendid Long Gallery through its expansive windows, creating a luminous promenade.

whitewashed by zealous Puritans in the 17th century, which protected the murals against decay. Also in the 15th century, a nine-panel alabaster reredos was built in the chapel and beautiful stained glass (dated 1427) installed.

At the end of the 15th century, Sir Henry Vernon built the Private Wing, including the Dining Room (originally known as the Parlour) and the Great Chamber above it. In the Dining Room, the painted ceiling (restored in 1926) includes black and red heraldic elements; in its wall panelling are carved medallions believed to represent Henry VII and his queen, Elizabeth of York.

'KING OF THE PEAK'

The celebrated oak-panelled Long Gallery, 110ft (34m) in length with beautiful oak panelling and carved walnut embellishments, was built by Sir George Vernon later in the 16th century. Sir George was celebrated for his hospitality and known as the 'King of the Peak'. Sir George's daughter, Dorothy, married John Manners, later Duke of Rutland. The house came to them, and the family lives there still.

GREAT HALL AT GREAT DIXTER

The cavernous Great Hall in the splendid timber-framed house of Great Dixter in East Sussex was built *c.*1440–54. Measuring 40 x 25ft (12 x 8m) and 31ft (9.5m) tall, it is one of England's largest surviving timber-framed halls. It has a splendid hammer-beam roof. Like Haddon Hall, Great Dixter was sensitively restored in the 20th century – in this case, by the architect Edwin Lutyens for owner Nathaniel Lloyd in 1910–11. Lutyens also designed a splendid topiary garden incorporating the manor's original farm buildings. Nathaniel Lloyd's sons, Quentin and Christopher, cared for the house and gardens respectively. Christopher, during whose period of care the gardens were internationally renowned and much visited, died on 27 January 2006.

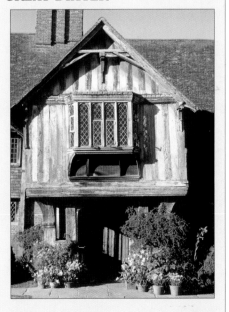

Above: The porch at Great Dixter is 16th century or earlier.

GLOSSARY

arrow slit Opening in castle wall through which defenders fired arrows at attackers. There were usually two types: a single vertical opening or a cross-shaped opening. The slits were not evenly spaced through the wall since to concentrate them in one area would have weakened the wall and also made it vulnerable to siege weapons.

bailey Area enclosed by the walls of a castle; also called 'ward'. Compare *motte*, the mound on which the *keep* was built. The most common early Norman castles consisted of a motte (with an initially wooden and later stone tower) and a bailey enclosed by an earthwork wall topped with a palisade. *See also* motte.

barbican A heavily fortified defensive structure, usually built out from the castle gateway. It often took the form of a double tower.

basilica In ancient Roman buildings, a big public hall.

bastide Walled town built alongside a castle. Originally a French term, but applied to castle-town developments such as Conwy in Wales.

bastion A projecting fortification on the curtain wall of a castle.

battlements A low defensive wall or parapet on the top of a castle's curtain wall or at the top of its towers, with indented sections (*embrasures or crenelles*) and raised parts (*merlons or cops*). Battlements originally protected members of the castle garrison on the sentry walk along the top of the wall; they were later used for decoration as householders sought to give homes the appearance of a castle.

bay Section of a house's outer wall, defined by vertical features, such as windows, columns and pilasters.

belvedere A raised building or room that commands a fine view.

Above: Windsor Castle.

broch Iron Age stone defensive tower found especially in northern Scotland.

bulwark A defensive fortification, usually made of earth.

burgh Anglo-Saxon fortified town, usually enclosed by earthenwork ramparts and a palisade. Also known as a burh or a borough.

buttery A storeroom for wines, so called because the wines were kept in butts (casks).

buttress A masonry structure built against a wall to support the wall.

citadel A fortress built in a strong defensive position within or close to a city and used to house the garrison that controlled the inhabitants. The citadel was often the garrison's last refuge when a city fell.

corbel Bracket in a wall supporting a vault or beam.

course A line or layer of stones or bricks in a wall.

crenellation The crenelle or part of a battlement that is indented, alongside the raised section or merlon. Defenders fired through the space provided by the crenellation, then leaned back to take cover behind the merlons.

cruciform In the shape of a cross.

curtain wall A castle's outer wall, linking its towers.

drawbridge A movable bridge across the castle *moat*. Drawbridges could be moved horizontally, or lifted vertically.

dressed stone Trimmed, smoothed and neatly cut stone.

drum tower A short round tower, usually built as a flanking tower for a barbican. See also *flanking tower*.

earthworks A bank of earth, usually dug for defence.

eave Part of a sloping roof that projects over the top of the wall.

enceinte The area enclosed by fortifications. The word was sometimes used to mean the perimeter of the fortification.

English bond In brickwork, the alternating use along a course of the brick ends ('headers') and the brick sides ('stretchers'). *See also* Flemish bond.

façade One of the main exteriors of a building. A façade usually contains an entrance.

facing A layer of one material over another.

firing gallery A room beneath the battlements in the castle walls or towers, with arrow slits in the stonework through which defenders could fire arrows and crossbow bolts at attackers.

flanking tower A tower built beside the castle gateway or in a strategic position along the curtain wall as a position from which defenders could provide flanking fire.

Flemish bond In brickwork, the use of the brick ends ('headers') throughout one course and then the brick sides ('stretchers') throughout the next. *See also* English bond.

gable The triangular profile at the end of a gable-roof (one with two sloping sides). Sometimes, also, a triangular extension above a doorway.

garderobe In castles and medieval houses, a privy or toilet. Alternatively, a walk-in wardrobe.

Gothic One of a series of styles in medieval architecture *c*.1150–*c*.1500. In England it applied principally to ecclesiastical architecture: there were no castles or fortified manor houses in the Gothic style.

half-timbered When the skeleton of a structure is made of wood and the remainder is made of brick or stone.

hall The main room in the castle or medieval house, used right up to Tudor times for dining and social occasions.

hammerbeam roof One in which the roof arch is supported by short beams that are set in the wall at the base of the roof.

keep The most strongly fortified part of a castle, usually containing the lord's apartments and often called the donjon (from French for 'lordship'). It functioned as a stronghold within the castle to which defenders could retreat if the outer *bailey* were captured by besiegers. The keep was usually a stone tower and usually stood on the *motte*, where there was one.

licence to crenellate Royal warrant allowing a lord or householder to construct a castle or add crenellations and other fortifications to a manor house.

linenfold panelling Decorative carving of wood, which is made to look like folded linen. A beautiful example is the linenfold panelling screen in the Big Hall at Compton Wynyates.

Long Gallery Feature of Tudor and especially Elizabethan-Jacobean houses, a long room was used as a promenade in bad weather and to display portraits and sculptures. There are fine examples at Hardwick Hall and Montacute.

Left: Conway Castle.

machicolation A section projecting from the outer face of a castle's curtain wall, with holes in the floor through which the castle's defenders threw rocks or poured oil on attackers. Strictly speaking, the machicolations were the openings in the floor. Also known as 'murder holes'.

moat A manmade ditch surrounding a castle or a town walls, usually filled with water.

motte Mound on which the keep of a castle was built. *See also* bailey.

mullion Vertical divider in a window containing more than one pane of glass (light). See also *transom*.

oriel window Projecting window supported by stone brackets or corbels.

palisade A defensive fence made from wooden stakes stuck into the ground.

portcullis A grill of wood or iron lowered for added defensive strength over a castle gateway.

postern Small, secondary gate (often concealed) in castle or town walls, Members of the garrison could use the postern to make inconspicuous exits and entries or to launch a surprise attack on a besieging force.

rampart A defensive earthenwork wall, topped with a palisade. In the plural the ramparts could describe the fortified walls of a castle or city.

ravelin A defensive fortification in the ditch of the moat, usually triangular in shape. Usually built near the gateway.

revetment Stone facing over a rubble wall.

Revival Use by patrons and architects of elements from an earlier architectural style. Examples include the late 18th-century/early 19th-century Greek Revival, and the several allied Victorian movements, such as the Norman, Tudor, Elizabethan and 'Jacobethan' Revivals.

rosette Flower motif in ornament.

rusticated Appearance of stone blocks that have been deliberately left rough to suggest strength.

Above: Beaumaris Castle.

screen A dividing wall that provides no actual structural support. In a medieval hall carved wooden screens were used to cover the passages to the kitchen.

shell keep A stone wall built around the top of the motte in a Norman motte and bailey castle. It was usually built to replace an earlier wooden wall.

shingles Wood pieces used in place of tiles.

solar A private chamber, usually on the first floor of a medieval-Tudor house, to which the lord and members of his family could retreat from the public space of the Great Hall. The solar was so called because it was fitted with large windows to allow in as much warming sunlight as possible. The lord and family members kept an eye on goings on in the Hall through 'squints' (hidden openings) in the intervening wall.

spur A sloping section added at the foot of a tower or castle wall. The spur made it harder for sapper to dig under and so undermine the walls, and for attackers to raise ladders against the wall. It also provided further protection against missiles. Also known as a talus.

squints (hidden openings) in a wall.

stockade An enclosure surrounded by stakes.

transom Horizontal divider in a window containing more than one pane of glass (light). See also *Mullion*.

turret A small tower, often built at the angles of a castle.

PROPERTY LISTINGS

All information was accurate at the time of going to press.

ALNWICK CASTLE
Alnwick, Northumberland
NE66 1NQ
01665 510777
www.alnwickcastle.com

ARUNDEL CASTLE
Arundel
West Sussex BN18 9AB
01903 883136
www.arundelcastle.org.uk

BALMORAL CASTLE
Balmoral, Ballater
Aberdeenshire AB35 5TB
013397 42534
www.balmoralcastle.com

BAMBURGH CASTLE
Bamburgh
Northumberland NE69 7DF
01668 214515
www.bamburghcastle.com

BEAULIEU
Brockenhurst
Hampshire SO42 7ZN
01590 612345
www.beaulieu.co.uk

BEAUMARIS CASTLE
Beaumaris
Anglesey LL58 8AP
01248 810361
www.beaumaris.com

BERKELEY CASTLE
Gloucestershire
GL13 9BQ
01453 810332
www.berkeley-castle.com

BERKHAMSTED CASTLE
Berkhamsted
St Albans
Hertfordshire
01223 582700
www.english-heritage.org.uk

BIGNOR ROMAN VILLA
Bignor, Pulborough
West Sussex RH20 1PH
01798 869259
www.romansinsussex.co.uk/sussex

BODIAM CASTLE
Bodiam, near Robertsbridge
East Sussex TN32 5UA
01580 830436
www.nationaltrust.org.uk

BOLSOVER CASTLE
Castle Street, Bolsover, Chesterfield,
Derbyshire S44 6PR
01246 856456
www.english-heritage.org.uk

BROCH OF GURNESS
Aikerness, Orkney
01856 751414
www.historic-scotland.gov.uk

BROUGHTON CASTLE
Broughton, near Banbury, Oxfordshire
OX15 5EB
01295 276070
www.broughtoncastle.com

CAERLAVEROCK CASTLE
Glencaple, Dumfries DG1 4RU
01387 770244
www.historic-scotland.gov.uk

Left: Manorbier Castle.

CAERLEON ROMAN FORT
High Street, Caerleon
Gwent NP18 1AE
01633 423134
www.museumwales.ac.uk/en/caerleon

CAERNARFON CASTLE
Castle Ditch
Caernarfon LL55 2AY
01286 677617
www.cadw.wales.gov.uk

CAERPHILLY CASTLE
Caerphilly CF8 1JL
029 2088 3143
www.cadw.wales.gov.uk

CAISTER CASTLE
Caister-on-Sea
Great Yarmouth
Norfolk NR30 5SN
01572 787251
www.greateryarmouth.co.uk/caister
_castle.htm

CAMBER CASTLE
Camber, near Rye
East Sussex TN31 7RS
01797 223862
www.english-heritage.org.uk

CARDIFF CASTLE
Castle Street
Cardiff CF10 3RB
029 2087 8100
www.cardiffcastle.com

CARISBROOKE CASTLE
Newport
Isle of Wight PO30 1XY
01983 522107
www.english-heritage.org.uk

CASTELL COCH
Tongwynlais
Cardiff CF4 7JS
029 2081 0101
www.cadw.wales.gov.uk

CASTLE OF MEY
Thurso, Caithness KW14 8XH
01847 851473
www.castleofmey.org.uk

CAWDOR CASTLE
Nairn IV12 5RD
01667 404401
www.cawdorcastle.com

CHEPSTOW CASTLE
Chepstow, Gwent
01291 624065
www.cadw.wales.gov.uk

CHESTERS ROMAN FORT
Chollerford, near Hexham,
Northumberland NE46 4EU
01434 681379
www.english-heritage.org.uk

CONWAY CASTLE
Conwy LL32 8AY
0149 2592358
www.conwy.com

DEAL CASTLE
Victoria Road, Deal, Kent CT14 7BA
01304 372762
www.english-heritage.org.uk

DOVER CASTLE
Dover, Kent CT16 1HU
01304 211067
www.english-heritage.org.uk

DUNFERMLINE ABBEY AND PALACE
Dunfermline, Fife
01383 739026
www.historic-scotland.gov.uk

EDINBURGH CASTLE
Castlehill, Edinburgh EH12NG
0131 225 9846
www.historic-scotland.gov.uk
or www.edinburghcastle.gov.uk

EILEAN DONAN CASTLE
Dornie, Kyle of Localsh
Wester Ross IV40 8DX
01599 555202
www.eileandonancastle.com

ELTHAM PALACE
Court Yard, Eltham
London SE9 5QE
020 8294 2548
www.english-heritage.org.uk

FALKLAND PALACE
Falkland
KY15 7BU
0844 4932186
www.nts.org.uk

FISHBOURNE ROMAN PALACE
Salthill Road
Fishbourne
Chichester
West Sussex PO19 3QS
01243 785859
www.sussexpast.co.uk

FRAMLINGHAM CASTLE
Framlingham, Suffolk IP13 9BT
01728 724189
www.english-heritage.org.uk

GLAMIS CASTLE
Glamis by Forfar, Angus DD8 1RJ
01307 840393
www.glamis-castle.co.uk

GOODRICH CASTLE
Ross-on-Wye, Herefordshire
HR9 6HY
01600 890538
www.english-heritage.org.uk

GREAT DIXTER HOUSE
Northiam, Rye
East Sussex TN31 6PH
01797 252878
www.greatdixter.co.uk

HADDON HALL
Bakewell, Derbyshire DE45 1LA
01629 812855
www.haddonhall.co.uk

HARDWICK OLD HALL
Doe Lea, Chesterfield
Derbyshire S44 5QJ
01246 850431
www.english-heritage.org.uk

Above: Beaumaris Castle.

HARLECH CASTLE
Harlech LL46 2YH
01766 780552
www.harlech.com

HELLENS
Much Marcle
Ledbury
Herefordshire
HR8 2LY
01531 660504
www.hellensmanor.com

HERSTMONCEUX CASTLE
Hailsham
Sussex BN27 1RN
01323 834444
www.herstmonceux-castle.com

HEVER CASTLE
Hever, Edenbridge
Kent TN8 7NG
01732 865224
www.hever-castle.co.uk

HOLYROODHOUSE PALACE
Canongate
The Royal Mile
EH8 8DX
0131 556 5100
www.royalcollection.org.uk

HOUSESTEADS ROMAN FORT
near Haydon Bridge
Northumberland NE47 6NN
01434 344363
www.nationaltrust.org.uk

IGHTHAM MOTE
Mote Road, Ivy Hatch
Sevenoaks, Kent TN15 0NT
01732 810378
www.nationaltrust.org.uk

JEWEL TOWER
Abingdon Street
Westminster
London SW1P 3JX
020 7222 2219
www.english-heritage.or.uk

KENILWORTH CASTLE
Kenilworth
Warwickshire CV8 1NE
01926 852078
www.english-heritage.org.uk

KIDWELLY CASTLE
Kidwelly
West Glamorgan SA17 5BG
01554 890104
www.cadw.wales.gov.uk

KILLYLEAGH CASTLE
Killyleagh, Downpatrick, Co Down
BT30 9QA
028 4482 8261
www.killyleaghcastle.com

KNOLE
Knole, Sevenoaks
Kent TN15 0RP
01732 462100
www.nationaltrust.org.uk

LAYER MARNEY TOWER
near Colchester
Essex CO5 9US
01206 330784
www.layermarneytower.co.uk

LEEDS CASTLE
Maidstone
Kent ME17 1PL
01622 765400
www.leeds-castle.com

LEWES CASTLE
169 High Street
Lewes, Sussex
BN7 1YE
01273 486290
www.sussexpast.co.uk

LINLITHGOW PALACE
Linlithgow
West Lothian EH49 7AL
01506 842896
www.historic-scotland.gov.uk

LUDLOW CASTLE
Castle Square, Ludlow
Shropshire
SY8 1AY
01584 873355
www.ludlowcastle.com

LULLINGSTONE ROMAN VILLA
Lullingstone Lane
Eynsford
Kent DA4 0JA
01322 863467
www.english-heritage.org.uk

MIDDLEHAM CASTLE
Castle Hill, Middleham
Leyburn,
North Yorkshire DL8 4QR
01969 623899
www.english-heritage.org.uk

MUNCASTER CASTLE
Ravenglass, Cumbria CA18 1RQ
01229 717614
www.muncaster.co.uk

NORTON CONYERS
Near Ripon, North Yorkshire
HG4 5EQ
01765 640333
www.ripon.org/norton.php

Left: Edinburgh Castle.

Above: Eilean Donan Castle.

NOTTINGHAM CASTLE
Nottingham NG1 6EL
0115 9153700
www.nottinghamcity.gov.uk/sitemap/
leisure_and_culture/museumsandgalleries
/nottinghamcastle.htm

ORFORD CASTLE
Orford, Woodbridge, Suffolk IP12 2ND
01394 450472
www.english-heritage.org.uk

PALACE OF WESTMINSTER
London SW1A 0AA
020 7219 3000
www.parliament.uk/parliament/guide/
palace.htm

PEMBROKE CASTLE
Pembroke SA71 4LA
01646 681510
www.pembrokecastle.co.uk

PENRHYN CASTLE
Bangor LL57 4HN
01248 353084
www.nationaltrust.org.uk

PENSHURST PLACE
Penshurst, near Tonbridge
Kent TN11 8DG
01892 870307
www.penshurstplace.com

PEVENSEY CASTLE
Pevensey, Sussex BN24 5LE
01323 762604
www.english-heritage.org.uk

PEVERIL CASTLE
Market Place, Castleton
Hope Valley
Derbyshire S33 8WQ
01433 620613
www.english-heritage.org.uk

PORTCHESTER CASTLE
Portsmouth
Hampshire PO16 9QW
02392 378291
www.english-heritage.org.uk

PORTLAND CASTLE
Castletown
Portland
Weymouth
Dorset DT5 1AZ
01305 820539
www.english-heritage.org.uk

POWIS CASTLE
near Welshpool SY21 8RF
01938 551929
www.nationaltrust.org.uk

RABY CASTLE
Staindrop, Darlington
Co Durham DL2 3AH
01833 660202
www.rabycastle.com

RAGLAN CASTLE
Raglan NP5 2BT
01291 690228
www.cadw.wales.gov.uk

RHUDDLAN CASTLE
Castle Gate, Castle Street
Rhuddlan LL18 5AD
01745 590777
www.cadw.wales.gov.uk

RICHMOND CASTLE
Tower Street, Richmond
North Yorskhire DL10 4QW
01748 822493
www.english-heritage.org.uk

ROCHESTER CASTLE
The Lodge, Rochester-upon-Medway,
Medway ME1 1SW
01634 402276
www.english-heritage.org.uk

ST MAWES CASTLE
St Mawes
Cornwall TR2 3AA
01326 270526
www.english-heritage.org.uk

ST MICHAEL'S MOUNT
Marazion, near Penzance
Cornwall TR17 0EF
01736 710507
www.stmichaelsmount.co.uk

SCONE PALACE
Perth PH2 6BD
01738 552300
www.scone-palace.net

STIRLING CASTLE
Castle Wynd, Stirling FK8 1EJ
01786 450000
www.historic-scotland.gov.uk

STOKESAY CASTLE
near Craven Arms
Shropshire SY7 9AH
01588 672544
www.english-heritage.org.uk

SUDELEY CASTLE
Winchcombe, Gloucestershire
GL54 5JD
01242 604357
www.sudeleycastle.co.uk

TATTERSHALL CASTLE
Tattershall, Lincoln LN4 4LR
01526 342543
www.nationaltrust.org.uk

Left: Castle Urquhart.

Above: Corfe Castle.

TINTAGEL CASTLE
Tintagel, Cornwall PL34 0HE
01840 770328
www.english-heritage.org.uk

TOWER OF LONDON
London EC3N 4AB
0870 756 6060
www.hrp.org.uk

WALMER CASTLE
Walmer, Deal, Kent CT14 7LJ
01304 364288
www.english-heritage.org.uk

WARWICK CASTLE
Warwick CV34 4QU
0870 442 2000
www.warwick-castle.co.uk

WINCHESTER CASTLE GREAT HALL
Winchester SO23 8PJ
01962 846476
www.hants.gov.uk/greathall

WINDSOR CASTLE
Windsor, Berkshire SL4 1NJ
020 7766 7304
www.royalcollection.org.uk

WOLLATON HALL
Wollaton, Nottingham NG8 2AE
0115 915 3900
www.nottinghamcity.gov.uk/sitemap/
leisure_and_culture/museumsandgalleries
/wollatonhall.htm

INDEX

ACKNOWLEDGEMENTS

Alamy: AA World Travel Library: 73t; Tim Ayers: 18-19; Sandra Baker: 6b; Peter Barritt: 60b; Bildarchiv Monheim GmbH: 7t, 21t; BL Images Ltd: 55b; Michael Booth: 31t, 58–9, 70b; David Cattanach: 81t; Adrian Chinery: 85t; Gary Cook: 57b; Guy Edwardes: 6t, 69t; Bernie Epstein: 29b; Robert Estall: 40b; eye35.com: 9t; B E Eyley: 68bl; Paul Felix: 53t; Chris Gloag: 60t, 61b, 61t; Duncan Hale-Sutton: 78t; Andrew Harris: 7b; Jeremy Hoare: 38b; Doug Houghton: 20b; Michael Jenner: 34t, 70t; Hywel Jones: 69b; Iconotec: 14, 71b; iX Images: 31b; Mike Kipling: 42b, 43b, 66t; Liquid Light: 47t, 55t; Pedro Luz Cunha: 40t; David Lyons: 29t; Manor Photography: 39tr; David Millichope: 54b; David Newham: 80b, 77t; David Norton: 3; one-image photography: 50t; Derek Payne: 65t; The Photolibrary Wales: 52b; David Poole: 10–11; Rob Rayworth: 36-7, 89; David Reed: 84t; Matthew Richardson: 76t; Rolf Richardson: 45; David Rowland: 73br & bl; Stephen Saks : 79b; ShelbyImages.com: 44t; Simmons Aerofilms: 20t; Skyscan: 21bl, 25t, 34b, 46b, 54t; Howard Taylor: 26b; Travel Ink: 50b; Darryl Webb: 15b, 41bl; www.white-windmill.co.uk: 72b; Worldwide Picture Library: 32t, 71t.

The Art Archive: 16b, 27t & b, 49t, 86t; Bodleian Library 16t /British Library 17bl /British Library/ HarperCollins Publishers 17t /Dagli Orti 17br; Jarrold Publishing: 2, 8b, 22t, 26t, 38t, 39tl, 67t; Musée de la Tapisserie/Dagli Orti: 23b; Musée du Chateau de Versailles/Dagli Orti: 78b.
Berkeley Castle Charitable Trust: 68br.
The Bridgeman Archive: © Ashmolean Museum: 21br; Hedingham Castle: 32b; © Bronte Parsonage Museum, Haworth: 83bl; © Chetham's Library, Manchester: 24t; J. Collins & Son Fine Paintings, Devon: 30b; Longleat House: 62t; © Mallett Gallery, London: 33b; Roy Miles Fine Paintings: 67b; © Newport Museum and Art Gallery: 35b, 48; Society of Antiquaries, London: 42t; Stapleton Collection, Private Collection: 46t; Topham Picture-point, Compton Wynyates: Penshurst Place: 62t; © Walters Art Museum, Baltimore: 44b.
Jonathan Buckley: 87b.
Cadw. Crown Copyright: 48b, 49b, 51t, 52t, 56t.
Corbis: Adam Woolfitt: 65b.
Lucy Doncaster: 10b.
© **EHS Built Heritage**: 39t, 41br, 41t.
Mary Evans Picture Library: 77b.
Tim Graham Picture Library: 82b.

Karita Guiney: 4m&r, 15t, 56b, 57tl, 9tl.
Haddon Hall: 86bl, 86br, 87tr, 87tl.
Leeds Castle: 64t.
Norton Conyers: 83t, 83br.
© **Penshurst Place**: 63b.
Pictures of Britain: John Blake: 9b; Dorothy Burrows: 23t, 28c, 53b; Brian Gibbs: 74–75; Ron Gregory: 82t; John Husband: 22b; Vera Hunter: 33t, 51b, 72t; John Larkin: 84b; Deryck Lister Hallam: 12m, 43t; Tom Parker: 35t; Adina Tovy: 1, 24b, 30t, 47b; Jeffery Whitelaw: 76b.
Rex Features: M. Nicolaou: 85b; J. Turner: 64b. © **David Sellman**/Penshurst Place: 62b.
Joy Wotton: 8t, 12tl, 90, 91, 93.
Peter Wotton: 3, 5l & m, 10t, 11b, 12tr, 28b, 68t, 80t, 81b, 96